Karen Armstrong spent seven years as a Roman Catholic nun, an experience she recollected in her best-selling autobiography, *Through the Narrow Gate*. She is the author of the worldwide best-seller *A History of God* (which has now appeared in more than thirty languages), the highly acclaimed *History of Jerusalem* and, most recently, *The Bible: A Biography*. She is an instructor at the Leo Baeck College in London and in 1999 received the Muslim Public Affairs Council Media Award.

By Karen Armstrong

Through the Narrow Gate
The First Christian: Saint Paul's Impact on Christianity
Beginning the World
Tongues of Fire: An Anthology of Religious and Poetic Experience
The Gospel According to Woman: Christianity's Creation of the Sex War in the West
Holy War: The Crusades and their Impact on Today's World
Muhammad: A Biography of the Prophet
The English Mystics of the Fourteenth Century
The End of Silence: Women and the Priesthood
A History of God: The 4000-Year Quest of Judaism, Christianity and Islam
A History of Jerusalem: One City, Three Faiths
In the Beginning: A New Interpretation of Genesis
Islam: A Short History
Buddha
The Battle for God: Fundamentalism in Judaism, Christianity and Islam
Faith After September 11th
The Spiral Staircase: My Climb Out of Darkness
A Short History of Myth
Muhammad: A Prophet For Our Time
The Great Transformation: The Beginning of Our Religious Traditions
The Bible: A Biography

BUDDHA

KAREN ARMSTRONG

PHOENIX

A PHOENIX PAPERBACK

First published in Great Britain in 2000
by Weidenfeld & Nicolson
This paperback edition published in 2002
by Phoenix,
an imprint of Orion Books Ltd,
Orion House, 5 Upper St Martin's Lane,
London WC2H 9EA

An Hachette UK Company

First published in the USA in 2000
by Viking/Penguin

A CIP catalogue record for this book
is available from the British Library.

Printed and bound in Great Britain by
Clays Ltd, St Ives plc

The Orion Publishing Group's policy is to use papers that are natural, renewable and recyclable products and made from wood grown in sustainable forests. The logging and manufacturing processes are expected to conform to the environmental regulations of the country of origin.

www.orionbooks.co.uk

For Lindsey Armstrong, my Buddhist sister

CONTENTS

INTRODUCTION

Some Buddhists might say that to write a biography of Siddhatta Gotama is a very un-Buddhist thing to do. In their view, no authority should be revered, however august; Buddhists must motivate themselves and rely on their own efforts, not on a charismatic leader. One ninth-century master, who founded the Lin-Chi line of Zen Buddhism, even went so far as to command his disciples, 'If you meet the Buddha, kill the Buddha!' to emphasize the importance of maintaining this independence from authority figures. Gotama might not have approved of the violence of this sentiment, but throughout his life he fought against the cult of personality, and endlessly deflected the attention of his disciples from himself. It was not his life and personality but his teaching that was important. He believed that he had woken up to a truth that was inscribed in the deepest structure of existence. It was a *dhamma;* the word has a wide range of connotations, but originally it denoted a fundamental law of life for gods, humans and animals alike. By discovering this truth, he had become enlightened and had experienced a profound inner transformation; he had won peace and immunity in the midst of life's suffering. Gotama had thus become a Buddha, an Enlightened or Awakened One.

Any one of his disciples could achieve the same enlightenment if he or she followed this method. But if people started to revere Gotama the man, they would distract themselves from their task, and the cult could become a prop, causing an unworthy dependence that could only impede spiritual progress.

The Buddhist scriptures are faithful to this spirit and seem to tell us little about the details of Gotama's life and personality. It is obviously difficult, therefore, to write a biography of the Buddha that will meet modern criteria, because we have very little information that can be considered historically sound. The first external evidence that a religion called Buddhism existed comes from inscriptions made by King Aṣoka, who ruled the Mauryan state in North India from about 269 to 232 B.C.E. But he lived some two hundred years after the Buddha. As a result of this dearth of reliable fact, some Western scholars in the nineteenth century doubted that Gotama had been a historical figure. They claimed that he had simply been a personification of the prevailing Sāṃkhya philosophy or a symbol of a solar cult. Yet modern scholarship has retreated from this skeptical position, and argues that even though little in the Buddhist scriptures is what is popularly known as 'gospel truth,' we can be reasonably confident that Siddhatta Gotama did indeed exist and that his disciples preserved the memory of his life and teachings as well as they could.

When trying to find out about the Buddha, we are dependent upon the voluminous Buddhist scriptures, which have been written in various Asian languages and take up several shelves in a library. Not surprisingly, the story of the composition of this large body of texts is complex and the status of its various parts much disputed. It is generally agreed that the most useful texts are those written in Pāli, a north

Indian dialect of uncertain provenance, which seems to have been close to Magadhan, the language that Gotama himself may have spoken. These scriptures were preserved by Buddhists in Sri Lanka, Burma and Thailand who belonged to the Theravāda school. But writing was not common in India until the time of Aṣoka, and the Pāli Canon was orally preserved and probably not written down until the first century B.C.E. How were these scriptures composed?

It seems that the process of preserving the traditions about the Buddha's life and teaching began shortly after his death in 483 (according to the traditional Western dating). Buddhist monks at this time led itinerant lives; they wandered around the cities and towns of the Ganges plain and taught the people their message of enlightenment and freedom from suffering. During the monsoon rains, however, they were forced off the road and congregated in their various settlements, and during these monsoon retreats, the monks discussed their doctrines and practices. Shortly after the Buddha died, the Pāli texts tell us that the monks held a council to establish a means of assessing the various extant doctrines and practices. It seems that about fifty years later, some of the monks in the eastern regions of North India could still remember their great Teacher, and others started to collect their testimony in a more formal way. They could not yet write this down, but the practice of yoga had given many of them phenomenally good memories, so they developed ways of memorizing the discourses of the Buddha and the detailed rules of their Order. As the Buddha himself had probably done, they set some of his teachings in verses and may even have sung them; they also developed a formulaic and repetitive style (still present in the written texts) to help the monks learn these discourses by heart. They divided the sermons and regulations into distinct but overlapping bodies of material, and certain monks were assigned the task of committing one of these anthologies to memory and passing it on to the next generation.

About a hundred years after the Buddha's death, a Second Council was held, and by this time it seems that the texts had reached the form of the present Pāli Canon. It is often called the *Tipiṭaka* ('Three Baskets') because later, when the scriptures were written down, they were kept in three separate receptacles: the Basket of Discourses (*Sutta Piṭaka*), the Basket of Disciplines (*Vinaya Piṭaka*), and a miscellaneous body of teachings. Each of these three 'Baskets' was subdivided as follows:

[1] *Sutta Piṭaka,* which consists of five 'collections' (*nikāyas*) of sermons, delivered by the Buddha:

[i] *Dīgha Nikāya,* an anthology of thirty-four of the longest discourses, which focus on the spiritual training of the monks, on the duties of the laity, and on various aspects of the religious life in India in the fifth century B.C.E. But there is also an account of the Buddha's qualities (*Sampasādaniya*) and of the last days of his life (*Mahāparinibbāṇa*).

[ii] *Majjhima Nikāya,* an anthology of 152 middle-length sermons (*suttas*). These include a large number of stories about the Buddha, his struggle for enlightenment and his early preaching, as well as some of the core doctrines.

[iii] *Saṁyutta Nikāya:* a collection of five series of *suttas,* which are divided according to subject, on such matters as the Eightfold Path and the makeup of the human personality.

[iv] *Aṇguttara Nikāya,* which has eleven divisions of *suttas,* most of which are included in other parts of the scriptures.

[v] *Khuddaka-Nikāya,* a collection of minor works, which include such popular texts as the *Dhammapada,* an anthology of the Buddha's epigrams and short poems; the *Udāna,* a collection of some of the Buddha's maxims, composed mostly in verse, with introductions telling how each one came to be delivered; the *Sutta-Nipāta,* another collection of verses, which includes some legends about the Buddha's life; and the *Jātaka,* stories about the former lives of the Buddha and his companions, to illustrate how a person's *kamma* ('actions') have repercussions in their future existences.

[2] *The Vinaya Piṭaka,* the Book of Monastic Discipline, which codifies the rules of the Order. It is divided into three parts:

[i] the *Sutta Vibhanga,* which lists the 227 offenses which must be confessed at the fortnightly chapter, with a commentary explaining how each rule came to be made.

[ii] The *Khandhakhas,* which are subdivided into the *Mahāvagga* (the Great Series), and the *Cullavagga* (the Lesser Series), which give rules for admission to the Order, the way of life and the ceremonies, also with commentaries, explaining the incidents which gave rise to the rules. These commentaries introducing each rule have preserved important legends about the Buddha.

[iii] The *Parivāra:* summaries and classifications of the rules.

The 'Third Basket' (*Abhidhamma Piṭaka*) deals with philosophical and doctrinal analyses and has little of interest to the biographer.

After the Second Council, there was a schism in the Buddhist movement, which split up into a number of sects.

Each school took these old texts but rearranged them to fit its own teaching. In general, it seems that no material was discarded, even though there were additions and elaborations. Clearly the Pāli Canon, the scripture of the Theravāda school, was not the only version of the *Tipiṭaka,* but it was the only one to survive in its entirety. Yet fragments of some lost Indian material can be found in later translations of the scriptures into Chinese, or in the Tibetan scriptures, which give us our earliest collection of Sanskrit texts. So even though these translations were composed in the fifth and sixth centuries C.E., about a thousand years after the Buddha's death, some parts are as old as and corroborate the Pāli Canon.

From this brief account, several points emerge that will affect the way we approach this scriptural material. First, the texts purport to be simple collections of the Buddha's own words, with no authorial input from the monks. This mode of oral transmission precludes individualistic authorship; these scriptures are not the work of a Buddhist equivalent of the evangelists known as Matthew, Mark, Luke and John, each of whom gives his own idiosyncratic view of the Gospel. We know nothing about the monks who compiled and edited all these texts, nor about the scribes who later committed them to writing. Second, the Pāli Canon is bound to reflect the viewpoint of the Theravādin school, and may have slanted the originals for polemical purposes. Third, despite the excellence of the monks' yoga-trained memories, this mode of transmission was inevitably flawed. Much material was probably lost, some was misunderstood, and the monks' later views were doubtless projected onto the Buddha. We have no means of distinguishing which of these stories and sermons are authentic and which are invented. The scriptures do not provide us with information that will satisfy the criteria of modern scientific history. They can only claim to reflect a legend about Gotama that existed some three generations after his death, when the Pāli Canon took definitive form. The later Tibetan and Chinese scriptures certainly contain ancient material, but they also represent a still later development of the legend. There is also the sobering fact that the oldest Pāli manuscript to have survived is only about 500 years old.

But we need not despair. The texts do contain historical material which seems to be reliable. We learn a great deal about North India in the fifth century B.C.E., which agrees with the scriptures of the Jains, who were contemporary with Buddha. The texts contain accurate references to the religion of the Vedas, about which the Buddhists who composed the later scriptures and the commentaries were largely ignorant; we learn about historical personages, such as King Bimbisāra of Magadha, about the emergence of city life, and about the political, economic and religious institutions of the period which agrees with the discoveries made by archeologists, philologists and historians. Scholars are now confident that some of this scriptural material probably does go back to the very earliest Buddhism. Today it is also difficult to accept the nineteenth-century view that the Buddha was simply an invention of the Buddhists. This mass of teachings all has a consistency and a coherence that point to a single original intelligence, and it is hard to see them as a corporate creation. It is not at all impossible that some of these words were really uttered by Siddhatta Gotama, even though we cannot be certain which they are.

Another crucial fact emerges from this description of the Pāli Canon: it contains no continuous narrative of the Buddha's life. Anecdotes are interspersed with the teaching and simply introduce a doctrine or a rule. Sometimes in his sermons, the Buddha tells his monks about his early life or his enlightenment. But there is nothing like the developed chronological accounts of the lives of Moses or Jesus in the Jewish and Christian scriptures. Later, Buddhists did write extended, consecutive biographies. We have the Tibetan *Lalita-Vistara* (third century C.E.) and the Pāli *Nidāna Kathā* (fifth century C.E.), which takes the form of a commentary on the *Jātaka* stories. The Pāli Commentaries on the Canon, put into their final form by the Theravādin scholar Buddhaghosa in the fifth century C.E., also helped readers to place the sporadic and unconsecutive events recounted in the Canon in some chronological order. But even these extended narratives have lacunae. They contain almost no details about the forty-five years of the Buddha's teaching mission, after his enlightenment. The *Lalita-Vistara* ends with the Buddha's first sermon, and the *Nidāna Kathā* concludes with the foundation of the first Buddhist settlement in Sāvatthī, the capital of Kosala, at the outset of his preaching career. There are twenty years of the Buddha's mission about which we have no information at all.

All this would seem to indicate that those Buddhists who claim that the story of the historical Gotama is irrelevant are right. It is also true that the people of North India were not interested in history in our sense: they were more concerned about the meaning of historical events. As a result, the scriptures give little information about matters that most modern Western people would consider indispensable. We cannot even be certain what century the Buddha lived in. He was traditionally thought to have died in about 483 B.C.E., but Chinese sources would suggest that he could have died as late as 368 B.C.E. Why should anybody bother with the biography of Gotama, if the Buddhists themselves were so unconcerned about his life?

But this is not quite true. Scholars now believe that the later extended biographies were based on an early account of Gotama's life, composed at the time of the Second Council, which has been lost. Further, the scriptures show that the first Buddhists thought deeply about several crucial moments in Gotama's biography: his birth, his renunciation of normal domestic life, his enlightenment, the start of his teaching career, and his death. These were incidents of great importance. We may be in the dark about some aspects of Gotama's biography, but we can be confident that the general outline delineated by these key events must be correct. The Buddha always insisted that his teaching was based entirely on his own experience. He had not studied other people's views or developed an abstract theory. He had drawn his conclusions from his own life history. He taught his disciples that if they wanted to achieve enlightenment, they must abandon their homes, become mendicant monks, and practice the mental disciplines of yoga, as he had done. His life and teaching were inextricably combined. His was an essentially autobiographical philosophy, and the main contours of his life were described in the scriptures and commentaries as a model and an inspiration to other Buddhists. As he put it: 'He who sees me, sees the *dhamma* (the teaching), and he who sees the *dhamma* sees me.'

There is a sense in which this is true of any major religious figure. Modern New Testament scholarship has shown that we know far less about the historical Jesus than we thought we did. 'Gospel truth' is not as watertight as we assumed. But this has not prevented millions of people from modeling their lives on Jesus and seeing his path of compassion and suffering as leading to a new kind of life. Jesus certainly existed, but his story has been presented in the Gospels as a paradigm.

Christians have looked back to him when delving into the heart of their own problems. Indeed, it is only possible to comprehend Jesus fully if one has in some sense experienced personal transformation. The same is true of the Buddha, who, until the twentieth century, was probably one of the most influential figures of all time. His teaching flourished in India for 1,500 years, and then spread to Tibet, Central Asia, China, Korea, Japan, Sri Lanka and Southeast Asia. For millions of human beings, he has been the person who has epitomized the human situation.

It follows that understanding the Buddha's life, which is to an extent fused with his teaching, can help us all to understand the human predicament. But this cannot be the sort of biography which is usually written in the twenty-first century; it cannot trace what actually happened or discover controversial new facts about the Buddha's life, since there is not a single incident in the scriptures that we can honestly affirm to be historically true. What is historical is the fact of the legend, and we must take that legend whole, as it had developed at the time when the Pāli texts took their definitive shapes about a hundred years after the Buddha's death. Today, many readers will find aspects of this legend incredible: stories of gods and miracles are interspersed with the more mundane and historically probable events in Gotama's life. In modern historical criticism, it is usually a rule of thumb to discount miraculous events as later accretions. But if we do this with the Pāli Canon, we distort the legend. We cannot be certain that the more normal incidents are any more original to the legend than these so-called signs and wonders. The monks who evolved the Canon would certainly have believed in the existence of the gods, even though they saw them as limited beings and, as we shall see, were beginning to regard them as projections of human psychological states. They also believed that proficiency in yoga gave the yogin extraordinary 'miraculous' powers (*iddhi*). The yogic exercises trained the mind so that it could perform exceptional feats, just as the developed physique of the Olympic athlete gives him powers denied to ordinary mortals. People assumed that an expert yogin could levitate, read people's minds and visit other worlds. The monks who compiled the Canon would have expected the Buddha to be able to do these things, even though he himself had a jaundiced view of *iddhi* and felt that they should be avoided. As we shall see, the 'miracle stories' are often cautionary tales, designed to show the pointlessness of such spiritual exhibitionism.

Many of the stories recorded in the Pāli scriptures have an allegorical or symbolic meaning. The early Buddhists looked for significance, rather than historically accurate detail, in their scriptures. We shall also find that the later biographies, like the one found in the *Nidāna Kathā*, give alternative and more elaborate accounts of such incidents as Gotama's decision to leave his father's house, or his enlightenment, than the more sparse and technical narratives in the Pāli Canon. These later stories too are even more rich in mythological elements than the Canon: gods appear, the earth shakes, gates open miraculously. Again, it would be a mistake to imagine that these miraculous details were added to the original legend. These later consecutive biographies were probably based on that lost account of the Buddha's life which was composed about a century after his death, at the same time that the Canon took its definitive form. It would not have worried the early Buddhists that these overtly mythological tales were different from those in the Canon. They were simply a different interpretation of these events, bringing out their spiritual and psychological meaning.

But these myths and miracles show that even the Theravādin monks, who believed that the Buddha should simply be regarded as a guide and an exemplar, were beginning to see him as a superman. The more popular Mahāyāna school virtually deified Gotama. It used to be thought that the Theravāda represented a purer form of Buddhism and that the Mahāyāna was a corruption, but, again, modern scholars see both as authentic. The Theravāda continued to stress the importance of yoga and honored those monks who became Arahants, 'accomplished ones' who, like the Buddha, had achieved enlightenment. But the Mahāyāna, who revere the Buddha as an eternal presence in the lives of the people and as an object of worship, have preserved other values that are just as strongly emphasized in the Pāli texts, particularly the importance of compassion. They felt that the Theravāda was too exclusive and that the Arahants hugged enlightenment selfishly to themselves. They preferred to venerate the figures of the Bodhisattas, the men or women destined to become Buddhas but who deferred enlightenment in order to bring the message of deliverance to 'the many.' This, we shall see, was similar to Gotama's own perception of the role of his monks. Both schools had seized upon important virtues; both, perhaps, had also lost something.

Gotama did not want a personality cult, but paradigmatic individuals such as himself, Socrates, Confucius, and Jesus tend to be revered either as gods or as superhuman beings. Even the Prophet Muhammad, who always insisted that he was an ordinary human being, is venerated by Muslims as the Perfect Man, an archetype of the complete act of surrender (*islām*) to God. The immensity of the being and achievements of these people seems to defy ordinary categories. The Buddha legend in the Pāli Canon showed that this was happening to Gotama, and even though these miraculous stories cannot be literally true, they tell us something important about the way human beings function. Like Jesus, Muhammad, and Socrates, the Buddha was teaching men and women how to transcend the world and its suffering, how to reach beyond human pettiness and expediency and discover an absolute value. All were trying to make human beings more conscious of themselves and awaken them to their full potential. The biography of a person who has been canonized in this way cannot satisfy the standards of modern scientific history, but in studying the archetypal figure presented in the Pāli Canon and its related texts, we learn more about human aspiration and gain new insight into the nature of the human task. This paradigmatic tale delineates a different kind of truth about the human condition in a flawed and suffering world.

But a biography of the Buddha has other challenges. The Gospels present Jesus, for example, as a distinct personality with idiosyncracies; special turns of phrase, moments of profound emotion and struggle, irascibility and terror have been preserved. This is not true of the Buddha, who is presented as a type rather than as an individual. In his discourses we find none of the sudden quips, thrusts and witticisms that delight us in the speech of Jesus or Socrates. He speaks as the Indian philosophical tradition demands: solemnly, formally and impersonally. After his enlightenment, we get no sense of his likes and dislikes, his hopes and fears, moments of desperation, elation or intense striving. What remains is an impression of a transhuman serenity, self-control, a nobility that has gone beyond the superficiality of personal preference, and a profound equanimity. The Buddha is often compared to nonhuman beings – to animals, trees or plants – not because he is subhuman or inhumane, but because he has utterly transcended the selfishness that most of us regard as inseparable from our condition. The Buddha was trying to find a new way of being human. In the West, we prize individualism and self-expression, but this can easily degenerate into mere self-promotion. What we find in Gotama is a complete and breathtaking self-abandonment. He would not have been surprised to learn that the scriptures do not present him as a fully-rounded 'personality,' but would have said that our concept of personality was a dangerous delusion. He would have said that there was nothing unique about his life. There had been other Buddhas before him, each of whom delivered the same *dhamma* and had exactly the same experiences. Buddhist tradition claims that there have been twenty-five such enlightened human beings and that after the present historical era, when knowledge of this essential truth has faded, a new Buddha, called Metteyya, will come to earth and go through the same life-cycle. So strong is this archetypal perception of the Buddha that perhaps the most famous story about him in the *Nidāna Kathā,* his 'Going Forth' from his father's house, is said in the Pāli Canon to have happened to one of Gotama's predecessors, Buddha Vipassī. The scriptures were not interested in tracing Gotama's unique, personal achievements but in setting forth the path that all Buddhas, all human beings must take when they seek enlightenment.

The story of Gotama has particular relevance for our own period. We too are living in a period of transition and change, as was North India during the sixth and fifth centuries B.C.E. Like the people of North India, we are finding that the traditional ways of experiencing the sacred and discovering an ultimate meaning in our lives are either difficult or impossible. As a result, a void has been an essential part of the modern experience. Like Gotama, we are living in an age of political violence and have had terrifying glimpses of man's inhumanity to man. In our society too there are widespread malaise, urban despair and anomie, and we are sometimes fearful of the new world order that is emerging.

Many aspects of the Buddha's quest will appeal to the modern ethos. His scrupulous empiricism is especially congenial to the pragmatic tenor of our own Western culture, together with his demand for intellectual and personal independence. Those who find the idea of a supernatural God alien will also warm to the Buddha's refusal to affirm a Supreme Being. He confined his researches to his own human nature and always insisted that his experiences – even the supreme truth of Nibbāṇa – were entirely natural to humanity. Those who have become weary of the intolerance of some forms of institutional religiosity will also welcome the Buddha's emphasis on compassion and loving-kindness.

But the Buddha is also a challenge, because he is more radical than most of us. There is a creeping new orthodoxy in modern society that is sometimes called 'positive thinking.' At its worst, this habit of optimism allows us to bury our heads in the sand, deny the ubiquity of pain in ourselves and others, and to immure ourselves in a state of deliberate heartlessness to ensure our emotional survival. The Buddha would have had little time for this. In his view, the spiritual life cannot begin until people allow themselves to be invaded by the reality of suffering, realize how fully it permeates our whole experience, and feel the pain of all other beings, even those whom we do not find congenial. It is also true that most of us are not prepared for the degree of the Buddha's self-abandonment. We know that egotism is a bad thing; we know that all the great world traditions – not just Buddhism – urge us to transcend our selfishness. But when we seek liberation – in either a religious or secular guise – we really want to enhance our own sense of self. A good deal of what passes for religion is often designed to prop up and endorse the ego that the founders of the faith told us to abandon. We assume that a person like the Buddha, who has, apparently, and after a great struggle, vanquished all selfishness, will become inhuman, humorless and grim.

Yet that does not seem to have been true of the Buddha. He may have been impersonal, but the state he achieved inspired an extraordinary emotion in all who met him. The constant, even relentless degree of gentleness, fairness, equanimity, impartiality and serenity acquired by the Buddha touch a chord and resonate with some of our deepest yearnings. People were not repelled by his dispassionate calm, not daunted by his lack of preference for one thing, one person over another. Instead, they were drawn to the Buddha and flocked to him.

When people committed themselves to the regimen that he prescribed for suffering humanity, they said that they 'took refuge' with the Buddha. He was a haven of peace in a violent world of clamorous egotism. In one of the most moving stories in the Pāli Canon, a king in a state of acute depression took a drive one day through a park filled with huge tropical trees. He dismounted from his carriage and walked among their great roots, which were themselves as tall as an ordinary man, and noticed the way that they 'inspired trust and confidence.' 'They were quiet; no discordant voices disturbed their peace; they gave out a sense of being apart from the ordinary world, a place where one could take refuge from people' and find a retreat from the cruelties of life. Looking at these wonderful old trees, the king was reminded immediately of the

Buddha, jumped into his carriage and drove for miles until he reached the house where the Buddha was staying.[1] The search for a place apart, separate from the world and yet marvelously within it, that is impartial, utterly fair, calm and which fills us with the faith that, against all odds, there is value in our lives, is what many seek in the reality we call 'God.' In the person of the Buddha, who had gone beyond the limitations and partialities of selfhood, people seemed to find it in a human being. The life of the Buddha challenges some of our strongest convictions, but it can also be a beacon. We may not be able to practice the method he prescribed in its entirety, but his example illuminates some of the ways in which we can reach for an enhanced and more truly compassionate humanity.

Note. In quoting from the Buddhist scriptures, I have drawn on the translations made by other scholars. But I have paraphrased them myself and produced my own version to make them more accessible to the Western reader. Some key terms of Buddhism are now commonly used in ordinary English discourse, but we have usually adopted the Sanskrit rather than the Pāli forms. For the sake of consistency, I have kept to the Pāli, so the reader will find *kamma, dhamma* and Nibbāṇa, for example, instead of *karma, dharma* and Nirvana.

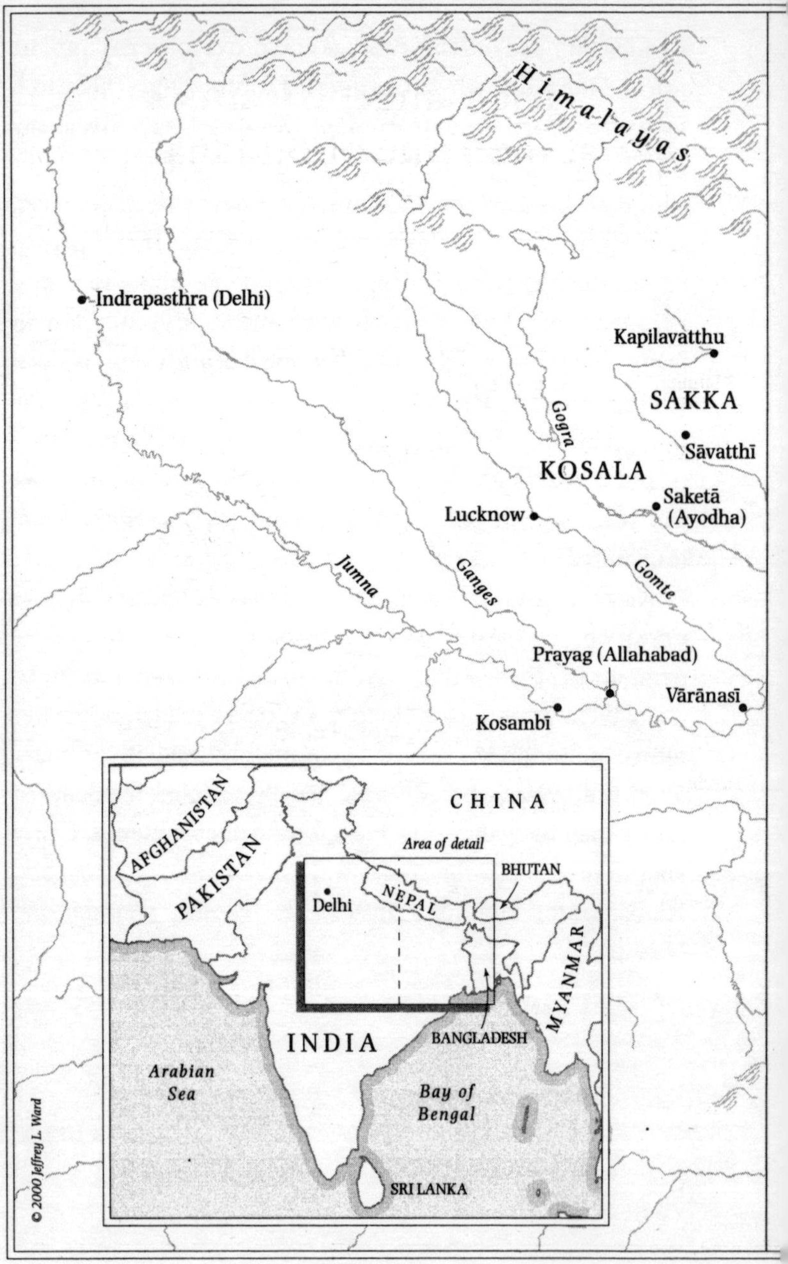
Himalayas
Indrapasthra (Delhi)
Kapilavatthu
SAKKA
Gogra
Sāvatthī
KOSALA
Saketā
(Ayodha)
Lucknow
Jumna
Ganges
Gomte
Prayag (Allahabad)
Vārānasī
Kosambī
AFGHANISTAN
PAKISTAN
CHINA
Area of detail
BHUTAN
Delhi
NEPAL
MYANMAR
INDIA
BANGLADESH
Arabian
Sea
Bay of
Bengal
SRI LANKA
© 2000 Jeffrey L. Ward

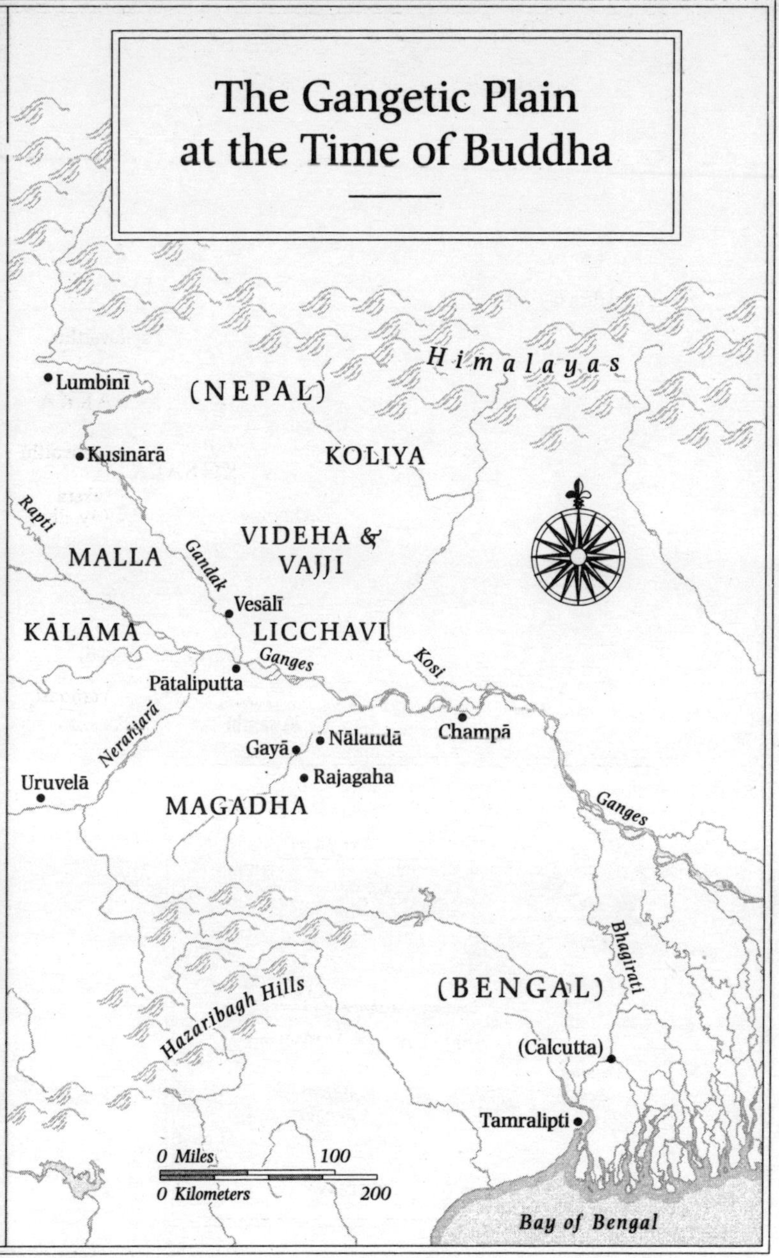
The Gangetic Plain
at the Time of Buddha
Himalayas
Lumbinī
(NEPAL)
Kusinārā
KOLIYA
Rapti
VIDEHA &
VAJJI
MALLA
Gandak
Vesālī
KĀLĀMA
LICCHAVI
Ganges
Kosi
Pātaliputta
Nerañjarā
Champā
Gayā
Nālandā
Uruvelā
Rajagaha
MAGADHA
Ganges
Bhagirati
(BENGAL)
Hazaribagh Hills
(Calcutta)
Tamralipti
0 Miles
100
0 Kilometers
200
Bay of Bengal

1 RENUNCIATION

ONE NIGHT TOWARD the end of the sixth century B.C.E., a young man called Siddhatta Gotama walked out of his comfortable home in Kapilavatthu in the foothills of the Himalayas and took to the road.[1] We are told that he was twenty-nine years old. His father was one of the leading men of Kapilavatthu and had surrounded Gotama with every pleasure he could desire; he had a wife and a son who was only a few days old, but Gotama had felt no pleasure when the child was born. He had called the little boy Rāhula, or 'fetter': the baby, he believed, would shackle him to a way of life that had become abhorrent.[2] He had a yearning for an existence that was 'wide open' and as 'complete and pure as a polished shell,' but even though his father's house was elegant and refined, Gotama found it constricting, 'crowded' and 'dusty.' A miasma of petty tasks and pointless duties sullied everything. Increasingly he had found himself longing for a lifestyle that had nothing to do with domesticity, and which the ascetics of India called 'homelessness.'[3] The thick luxuriant forests that fringed the fertile plain of the Ganges river had become the haunt of thousands of men and even a few women who had all shunned their families in order to seek what they called 'the holy life' (*brahmacariya*), and Gotama had made up his mind to join them.

It was a romantic decision, but it caused great pain to the people he loved. Gotama's parents, he recalled later, wept as they watched their cherished son put on the yellow robe that had become the uniform of the ascetics and shave his head and beard.[4] But we are also told that before he left, Sidhatta stole upstairs, took one last look at his sleeping wife and son, and crept away without saying goodbye.[5] It is almost as though he did not trust himself to hold true to his resolve should his wife beg him to stay. And this was the nub of the problem, since, like many of the forest-monks, he was convinced that it was his attachment to things and people which bound him to an existence that seemed mired in pain and sorrow. Some of the monks used to compare this kind of passion and craving for perishable things to a 'dust' which weighed the soul down and prevented it from soaring to the pinnacle of the universe. This may have been what Siddhatta meant when he described his home as 'dusty.' His father's house was not dirty, but it was filled with people who pulled at his heart and with objects that he treasured. If he wanted to live in holiness, he had to cut these fetters and break free. Right from the start, Siddhatta Gotama took it for granted that family life was incompatible with the highest forms of spirituality. It was a perception shared not only by the other ascetics of India, but also by Jesus, who would later tell potential disciples that they must leave their wives and children and abandon their aged relatives if they wanted to follow him.[6]

Gotama would not, therefore, have agreed with our current cult of 'family values.' Nor would some of his contemporaries or near-contemporaries in other parts of the world, such as Confucius (551–479) and Socrates (469–399), who were certainly not family-minded men, but who would, like Gotama himself, become key figures in the spiritual and philosophical development of humanity during this period. Why this rejectionism? The later Buddhist scriptures would evolve elaborate mythological accounts of Gotama's renunciation of domesticity and his 'Going Forth' into homelessness, and we shall consider these later in this chapter. But the earlier texts of the Pāli Canon give a starker version of the young man's decision. When he looked at human life, Gotama could see only a grim cycle of suffering, which began with the trauma of birth and proceeded inexorably to 'aging, illness, death, sorrow and corruption.'[7] He himself was no exception to this universal rule. At present he was young, healthy and handsome, but whenever he reflected on the suffering that lay ahead, all the joy and confidence of youth drained out of him. His luxurious lifestyle seemed meaningless and trivial. He could not afford to feel 'revolted' when he saw a decrepit old man or somebody who was disfigured by a loathsome illness. The same fate – or something even worse – would befall him and everybody he loved.[8] His parents, his wife, his baby son and his friends were equally frail and vulnerable. When he clung to them and yearned tenderly toward them, he was investing emotion in what could only bring him pain. His wife would lose her beauty, and little Rāhula could die tomorrow. To seek happiness in mortal, transitory things was not only irrational: the suffering in store for his loved ones as well as for himself cast a dark shadow over the present and took away all his joy in these relationships.

But why did Gotama see the world in such bleak terms? Mortality is a fact of life that is hard to bear. Human beings are the only animals who have to live with the knowledge that they will die one day, and they have always found this vision of extinction difficult to contemplate. But most of us manage to find some solace in the happiness and affection that is also part of the human experience. Some people simply bury their heads in the sand and refuse to think about the sorrow of the world, but this is an unwise course, because, if we are entirely unprepared, the tragedy of life can be devastating. From the very earliest times, men and women devised religions to help them cultivate a sense that our existence has some ultimate meaning and value, despite the dispiriting evidence to the contrary. But sometimes the myths and practices of faith seem incredible. People then turn to other methods of transcending the sufferings and frustrations of daily life: to art, music, sex, drugs, sport or philosophy. We are beings who fall very easily into despair, and we have to work very hard to create within ourselves a conviction that life is good, even though all around us we see pain, cruelty, sickness and injustice. When he decided to leave home, Gotama, one might think, appeared to have lost this ability to live with the unpalatable facts of life and to have fallen prey to a profound depression.

Yet that was not the case. Gotama had indeed become disenchanted with domestic life in an ordinary Indian household, but he had not lost hope in life itself. Far from it. He was convinced that there was a solution to the puzzle of existence, and that he could find it. Gotama subscribed to what has been called the 'perennial philosophy,' because it was common to all peoples in all cultures in the premodern world.[9] Earthly life was obviously fragile and overshadowed by death, but it did not constitute the whole of reality. Everything in the mundane world had, it was thought, its more powerful, positive replica in the divine realm. All that we experienced here below was modeled on an archetype in the celestial sphere;

the world of the gods was the original pattern of which human realities were only a pale shadow. This perception informed the mythology, ritual and social organizations of most of the cultures of antiquity and continues to influence more traditional societies in our own day. It is a perspective that is difficult for us to appreciate in the modern world, because it cannot be proved empirically and lacks the rational underpinning which we regard as essential to truth. But the myth does express our inchoate sense that life is incomplete and that this cannot be all there is; there *must* be something better, fuller and more satisfying elsewhere. After an intense and eagerly awaited occasion, we often feel that we have missed something that remains just outside our grasp. Gotama shared this conviction, but with an important difference. He did not believe that this 'something else' was confined to the divine world of the gods; he was convinced that he could make it a demonstrable reality in this mortal world of suffering, grief and pain.

Thus, he reasoned to himself, if there was 'birth, aging, illness, death, sorrow and corruption' in our lives, these sufferings states must have their positive counterparts; there must be another mode of existence, therefore, and it was up to him to find it. 'Suppose,' he said, 'I start to look for the *un*born, the *un*aging, *un*ailing, death*less,* sorrow*less, in*corrupt and supreme freedom from this bondage?' He called this wholly satisfactory state Nibbāṇa ('blowing out').[10] Gotama was convinced that it was possible to 'extinguish' the passions, attachments and delusions that cause human beings so much pain, rather as we snuff out a flame. To attain Nibbāṇa would be similar to the 'cooling' we experience after we recover from a fever: in Gotama's time, the related adjective *nibbuta* was a term in daily use to describe a convalescent. So Gotama was leaving home to find a cure for the sickness that plagues humanity and which fills men and women with unhappiness. This universal suffering which makes life so frustrating and miserable was not something that we were doomed to bear forever. If our experience of life was currently awry, then, according to the law of archetypes, there must be another form of existence that was *not* contingent, flawed and transient. 'There *is* something that has not come to birth in the usual way, which has neither been created and which remains undamaged,' Gotama would insist in later life. 'If it did not exist, it would be impossible to find a way out.'[11]

A modern person may smile at the naïveté of this optimism, and find the myth of eternal archetypes wholly incredible. But Gotama would claim that he *did* find a way out and that Nibbāṇa did, therefore, exist. Unlike many religious people, however, he did not regard this panacea as supernatural. He did not rely on divine aid from another world, but was convinced that Nibbāṇa was a state that was entirely natural to human beings and could be experienced by any genuine seeker. Gotama believed that he could find the freedom he sought right in the midst of this imperfect world. Instead of waiting for a message from the gods, he would search within himself for the answer, explore the furthest reaches of his mind, and exploit all his physical resources. He would teach his disciples to do the same, and insisted that nobody must take his teaching on hearsay. They must validate his solutions empirically, in their own experience, and find for themselves that his method really worked. They could expect no help from the gods. Gotama believed that gods existed, but was not much interested in them. Here again, he was a man of his time and culture. The people of India had worshipped gods in the past: Indra, the god of war; Varuna, the guardian of the divine order; Agni, the fire god. But by the sixth century, these deities had begun to recede from the religious consciousness of the most thoughtful people. They were not exactly regarded as worthless, but they had become unsatisfactory as objects of worship. Increasingly, people were aware that the gods could not provide them with real and substantial help. The sacrifices performed in their honor did not in fact alleviate human misery. More and more men and women decided that they must rely entirely on themselves. They believed that the cosmos was ruled by impersonal laws to which even the gods were subject. Gods could not show Gotama the way to Nibbāṇa; he would have to depend upon his own efforts.

Nibbāṇa was not, therefore, a place like the Christian Heaven to which a believer would repair after death. Very few people in the ancient world at this point hoped for a blissful immortality. Indeed, by Gotama's day, the people of India felt imprisoned eternally in their present painful mode of existence, as we can see from the doctrine of reincarnation, which had become widely accepted by the sixth century. It was thought that a man or a woman would be reborn after death into a new state that would be determined by the quality of their actions (*kamma*) in their present life. Bad *kamma* would mean that you would be reborn as a slave, an animal or a plant; good *kamma* would ensure a better existence next time: you could be reborn as a king or even as a god. But rebirth in one of the heavens was not a happy ending, because divinity was no more permanent than any other state. Eventually, even a god would exhaust the good *kamma* which had divinized him; he would then die and be reborn in a less advantageous position on earth. All beings were, therefore, caught up in an endless cycle of *saṃsāra* ('keeping going'), which propelled them from one life to another. It sounds like a bizarre theory to an outsider, but it was a serious attempt to address the problem of suffering, and can be seen as inherently more satisfactory than attributing human fate to the frequently erratic decisions of a personalized god, who often seems to ensure that the wicked prosper. The law of *kamma* was a wholly impersonal mechanism that applied fairly and without discrimination to everybody. But the prospect of living one life after another filled Gotama, like most other people in northern India, with horror.

This is perhaps difficult to understand. Today many of us feel that our lives are too short and would love the chance to do it all again. But what preoccupied Gotama and his contemporaries was not so much the possibility of rebirth as the horror of redeath. It was bad enough to have to endure the process of becoming senile or chronically sick and undergoing a frightening, painful death *once,* but to be forced to go through all this again and again seemed intolerable and utterly pointless. Most of the religious solutions of the day were designed to help people extricate themselves from *saṃsāra* and achieve a final release. The freedom of Nibbāṇa was inconceivable because it was so far removed from our everyday experience. We have no terms to describe or even to envisage a mode of life in which there is no frustration, sorrow or pain, and which is not conditioned by factors beyond our control. But Indian sages of Gotama's day were convinced that this liberation was a genuine possibility. Western people often describe Indian thought as negative and nihilistic. Not so. It was breathtakingly optimistic and Gotama shared this hope to the full.

When he left his father's house clad in the yellow robes of a mendicant monk who begged for his food, Gotama believed that he was setting out on an exciting adventure. He felt the lure of the 'wide open' road, and the shining, perfect state of 'homelessness.' Everybody spoke of the 'holy life' at this time as a noble quest. Kings, merchants and wealthy householders alike honored these *bhikkhus* ('almsmen') and vied with one another for the privilege of feeding them. Some became their regular patrons and disciples. This was no passing craze. The people of India can be as materialistic as anybody else, but they have a long tradition of venerating those who seek the spiritual, and they continue to support them. Still, there was a special urgency in the Ganges region in the late sixth century B.C.E. People did not regard the renunciants as feeble drop-outs. There was a spiritual crisis in the region. The sort of disillusion and anomie that Gotama had experienced was widespread, and people were desperately aware that they needed a new religious solution. The monk was thus engaged in a quest that would benefit his fellows, often at huge cost to himself. Gotama was often described in heroic imagery, suggesting strength, energy and mastery. He was compared to a lion, a tiger and a fierce elephant. As a young man, he was seen as a 'handsome nobleman, capable of leading a crack army or a troop of elephants.'[12] People regarded the ascetics as pioneers: they were exploring the realms of the spirit to bring succor to suffering men and women. As a result of the prevailing unrest, many yearned for a Buddha, a man who was 'enlightened,' who had 'woken up' to the full potential of humanity and would help others to find peace in a world that had suddenly become alien and desolate.

Why did the people of India feel this dis-ease with life? This malaise was not confined to the subcontinent, but afflicted people in several far-flung regions of the civilized world. An increasing number had come to feel that the spiritual practices of their ancestors no longer worked for them, and an impressive array of prophetic and philosophical geniuses made supreme efforts to find a solution. Some historians call this period (which extended from about 800 to 200 B.C.E.) the 'Axial Age' because it proved pivotal to humanity. The ethos forged during this era has continued to nourish men and women to the present day.[13] Gotama would become one of the most important and most typical of the luminaries of the Axial Age, alongside the great Hebrew prophets of the eighth, seventh and sixth centuries; Confucius and Lao Tzu, who reformed the religious traditions of China in the sixth and fifth centuries; the sixth-century Iranian sage Zoroaster; and Socrates and Plato (c. 427–327), who urged the Greeks to question even those truths which appeared to be self-evident. People who participated in this great transformation were convinced that they were on the brink of a new era and that nothing would ever be the same again.

The Axial Age marks the beginning of humanity as we now know it. During this period, men and women became conscious of their existence, their own nature and their limitations in an unprecedented way.[14] Their experience of utter impotence in a cruel world impelled them to seek the highest goals and an absolute reality in the depths of their being. The great sages of the time taught human beings how to cope with the misery of life, transcend their weakness, and live in peace in the midst of this flawed world. The new religious systems that emerged during this period – Taoism and Confucianism in China, Buddhism and Hinduism in India, monotheism in Iran and the Middle East, and Greek rationalism in Europe – all shared fundamental characteristics beneath their obvious differences. It was only by participating in this massive transformation that the various peoples of the world were able to progress and join the forward march of history.[15] Yet despite its great importance, the Axial Age remains mysterious. We do not know what caused it, nor why it took root only in three core areas: in China; in India and Iran; and in the eastern Mediterranean. Why was it that only the Chinese, Iranians, Indians, Jews and Greeks experienced these new horizons and embarked on this quest for enlightenment and salvation? The Babylonians and the Egyptians had also created great civilizations, but they did not evolve an Axial ideology at this point, and only participated in the new ethos later: in Islam or Christianity, which were restatements of the original Axial impulse. But in the Axial countries, a few men sensed fresh possibilities and broke away from the old traditions. They sought change in the deepest reaches of their beings, looked for greater inwardness in their spiritual lives, and tried to become one with a reality that transcended normal mundane conditions and categories. After this pivotal era, it was felt that only by reaching beyond their limits could human beings become most fully themselves.

Recorded history only begins in about 3000 B.C.E.; until that time we have little documentary evidence of the way human beings lived and organized their societies. But people always tried to imagine what the 20,000 years of prehistory had been like, and to root their own experience in it. All over the world, in every culture, these ancient days were depicted in mythology, which had no historical foundation but which spoke of lost paradises and primal catastrophes.[16] In the Golden Age, it was said, gods had walked the earth with human beings. The story of the Garden of Eden, recounted in the Book of Genesis, the lost paradise of the West, was typical: once upon a time, there had been no rift between humanity and the divine: God strolled in the garden in the cool of the evening. Nor were human beings divided from one another. Adam and Eve lived in harmony, unaware of their sexual difference or of the distinction between good and evil.[17] It is a unity that is impossible for us to imagine in our more fragmented existence, but in almost every culture, the myth of this primal concord showed that human beings continued to yearn for a peace and wholeness that they felt to be the proper state of humanity. They experienced the dawning of self-consciousness as a painful fall from grace. The Hebrew Bible calls this state of wholeness and completeness *shalōm;* Gotama spoke of Nibbāṇa and left his home in order to find it. Human beings, he believed, had lived in this peace and fulfillment before, but they had forgotten the path that led to it.

As we have seen, Gotama felt that his life had become meaningless. A conviction that the world was awry was fundamental to the spirituality that emerged in the Axial countries. Those who took part in this transformation felt restless – just as Gotama did. They were consumed by a sense of helplessness, were obsessed by their mortality and felt a profound terror of and alienation from the world.[18] They expressed this malaise in different ways. The Greeks saw life as a tragic epic, a drama in which they strove for *katharsis* and release. Plato spoke of man's separation from the divine, and yearned to cast off the impurity of our present state and achieve unity with the Good. The Hebrew prophets of the eighth, seventh and sixth centuries felt a similar alienation from God, and saw their political exile as symbolic of their spiritual condition. The Zoroastrians of Iran saw life as a cosmic battle between Good and Evil, while in China, Confucius lamented the darkness of his age, which had fallen away from the ideals of the ancestors. In India, Gotama and the forest monks were convinced that life was *dukkha:* it was fundamentally 'awry,' filled with pain, grief and sorrow. The world had become a frightening place. The Buddhist scriptures speak of the 'terror, awe and dread' that people experienced when they ventured outside the city and went into the woods.[19] Nature had become obscurely menacing, rather as it had become inimical to Adam and Eve after their lapse. Gotama did not leave home to commune happily with nature in the woods, but experienced a continuous 'fear and horror.'[20] If a deer approached or if the wind rustled in the leaves, he recalled later, his hair stood on end.

What had happened? Nobody has fully explained the sorrow that fueled Axial Age spirituality. Certainly men and women had experienced anguish before. Indeed, tablets have been found in Egypt and Mesopotamia from centuries before this time that express similar disillusion. But why did the experience of suffering reach such a crescendo in the three core Axial regions? Somc historians see the invasions of the nomadic Indo-European horsemen as a common factor in all these areas. These Āryan tribesmen came out of Central Asia and reached the Mediterranean by the end of the third millennium, were established in India and Iran by about 1200 B.C.E. and were in China by the end of the second millennium. They brought with them a sense of vast horizons and limitless possibilities, and, as a master race, had developed a tragically epic consciousness. They replaced the old stable and more primitive communities, but only after periods of intense conflict and distress, which might account for the Axial Age malaise.[21] But the Jews and their prophets had no contact with these Āryan horsemen, and these invasions occurred over millennia, whereas the chief Axial transformations were remarkably contemporaneous.

Moreover, the type of culture developed by the Āryans in India, for example, bore no relation to the creativity of the Axial Age. By 1000 B.C.E., the Āryan tribesmen had settled down and established agricultural communities in most regions of the subcontinent. They dominated Indian society to such an extent that we now know almost nothing about the indigenous, pre-Āryan civilization of the Indus valley. Despite the dynamism of its origins, however, Āryan India was static and conservative, like most pre-Axial cultures. It divided the people into four distinct classes, similar to the four estates which would develop later in feudal Europe. The *brahmins* were the priestly caste, with responsibility for the cult: they became the most powerful. The warrior *ksatriya* class was devoted to government and defense; the *vaiśya* were farmers and stockbreeders who kept the economy afloat; and the *sudras* were slaves or outcastes who were unable to assimilate into the Āryan system. Originally the four classes were not hereditary; native Indians could become *ksatriyas* or *brahmins* if they possessed the requisite skills. But by Gotama's time, the stratification of society had acquired a sacred significance and become immutable, since it was thought to mirror the archetypal order of the cosmos.[22] There was no possibility of changing this order by moving from one caste to another.

Āryan spirituality was typical of the ancient, pre-Axial religions, which were based on acceptance of the status quo, involved little speculative thought about the meaning of life and saw sacred truth as something that was given and unchangeable; not sought but passively received. The Āryans cultivated the drug soma, which put the *brahmins* into a state of ecstatic trance in which they 'heard' (*sruti*) the inspired Sanskrit texts known as the Vedas.[23] These were not thought to be dictated by the gods but to exist eternally and to reflect the fundamental principles of the cosmos. A universal law, governing the lives of gods and human beings alike, was also a common feature of ancient religion. The Vedas were not written down, since writing was unknown in the subcontinent. It was, therefore, the duty of the *brahmins* to memorize and preserve these eternal truths from one generation to another, passing down this hereditary lore from father to son, since this sacred knowledge put human beings in touch with *brahman,* the underlying principle that made the world holy and enabled it to survive. Over the centuries, Sanskrit, the language of the original Āryan tribesmen, was superseded by local dialects and became incomprehensible to everybody but the *brahmins* – a fact which inevitably enhanced the *brahmins'* power and prestige. They alone knew how to perform the sacrificial ritual prescribed in the Vedas, which was thought to keep the whole world in existence.

It was said that at the beginning of time, a mysterious Creator had performed a primal sacrifice that brought gods, humans and the entire cosmos into existence. This primeval sacrifice was the archetype of the animal sacrifices performed by the *brahmins,* which gave them power over life and death. Even the gods depended upon these sacrifices and would suffer if the ritual was not performed correctly. The whole of life therefore centered around these rites. The *brahmins* were clearly crucial to the cult, but the *ksatriyas* and *vaiśyas* also had important roles. Kings and noblemen paid for the sacrifices, and the *vaiśyas* reared the cattle as victims. Fire was of great importance in Vedic religion. It symbolized humanity's control over the forces of nature, and the *brahmins* carefully tended three sacred fires in shrines. Each householder also honored his own domestic hearth with family rites. On the 'quarter' (*uposatha*) days of each lunar month, special offerings were made to the sacred fire. On the eve of the *uposatha, brahmins* and ordinary householders alike would fast, abstain from sex and work, and keep night vigil at the hearth. It was a holy time, known as the *upavasatha,* when the gods 'dwelt near' the householder and his family beside the fire.[24]

Vedic faith was thus typical of pre-Axial religion. It did not develop or change; it conformed to an archetypal order and did not aspire to anything different. It depended upon external rites, which were magical in effect and intended to control the universe; it was based on arcane, esoteric lore known only to a few.[25] This deeply conservative spirituality sought security in a reality that was timeless and changeless. It was completely different from the new Axial ethos. One need only think of Socrates, who was never content to accept traditional certainties as final, however august they might be. He believed that instead of receiving knowledge from outside, like the *sruti* Vedas, each person must find the truth within his own being. Socrates questioned everything, infecting his interlocutors with his own perplexity, since confusion was the beginning of the philosophical quest. The Hebrew prophets overturned some of the old mythical certainties of ancient Israel: God was no longer automatically on the side of his people, as he had been at the time of the Exodus from Egypt. He would now use the Gentile nations to punish Jews, each of whom had a personal responsibility to act with justice, equity and fidelity. Salvation and survival no longer depended upon external rites; there would be a new law and covenant written in the heart of each of the people. God demanded mercy and compassion rather than sacrifice. Axial faith put the onus on the individual. Wherever they looked, as we have seen, the Axial sages and prophets saw exile, tragedy and *dukkha.* But the truth that they sought enabled them to find peace, despite cruelty, injustice and political defeat. We need only recall the luminous calm of Socrates during his execution by a coercive state. The individual would still suffer and die; there was no attempt to avert fate by the old magical means; but he or she could enjoy a calm in the midst of life's tragedies that gave meaning to existence in such a flawed world.

The new religions sought inner depth rather than magical control. The sages were no longer content with external conformity but were aware of the profound psychic inwardness that precedes action. Crucial was the desire to bring unconscious forces and dimly perceived truths into the light of day. For Socrates, men already knew the truth, but only as an obscure memory within; they had to awaken this knowledge and become fully conscious of it by means of his dialectical method of questioning. Confucius studied the ancient customs of his people, which had hitherto been taken for granted and had remained unexamined. Now the values that they enshrined must be consciously fostered in order to be restored to their original radiance. Confucius wanted to make explicit ideas which had previously been merely intuited, and put elusive, half-understood intimations into clear language. Human beings must study themselves, analyze the reasons for their failures and thus find a beauty and order in the world that was not rendered meaningless by the fact of death. The Axial sages scrutinized the old mythology and reinterpreted it, giving the old truths an essentially ethical dimension. Morality had become central to religion. It was by ethics, not magic, that humanity would wake up to itself and its responsibilities, realize its full potential and find release from the darkness that pressed in on all sides. The sages were conscious of the past, and believed that the world had gone awry because men and women had forgotten the fundamentals of existence. All were convinced that there was an absolute reality that transcended the confusions of this world – God, Nibbāṇa, the Tao, *brahman* – and sought to integrate it within the conditions of daily life.

Finally, instead of hugging a secret truth to themselves as the *brahmins* had done, the Axial sages sought to publish it abroad.[26] The prophets of Israel spoke to ordinary people in impassioned sermons and eloquent gestures. Socrates questioned everyone he met. Confucius traveled widely in an attempt to transform society, instructing the poor and humble as well as the nobility. These sages were determined to put their theories to the test. Scripture was no longer the private possession of a priestly caste, but became a way of transmitting the new faith to the multitude. Study and debate became important religious activities. There was to be no more blind acceptance of the status quo, and no automatic fealty to received ideas. Truth had to be made a reality in the lives of those who struggled to achieve it. We shall see how closely Gotama mirrored the values of the Axial Age, and how he brought his own special genius to bear on the human dilemma.

The Axial transformation was already well under way in India, however, when he left his home in Kapilavatthu. Historians and scholars note that all these innovative ideologies were created in the setting of the marketplace, which had acquired a new centrality in the sixth century B.C.E.[27] Power was passing from the old partnership of King and Temple to the merchants, who were developing a different kind of economy. These social changes certainly contributed to the spiritual revolution, even if they cannot fully explain it. The market economy also undermined the status quo: merchants could no longer defer obediently to the priests and aristocracy. They had to rely on themselves and be prepared to be ruthless in business. A new urban class was coming into being, and it was powerful, thrusting, ambitious and determined to take its destiny into its own hands. It was clearly in tune with the newly emerging spiritual ethos. The plain around the river Ganges in North India, like the other Axial regions, was undergoing this economic transformation during Gotama's lifetime. By the sixth century, the essentially rural society that had been established by the Āryan invaders so long ago was being transformed by the new iron-age technology, which enabled farmers to clear the dense forests and thus open up new land for cultivation. Settlers poured into the region, which became densely populated and highly productive. Travelers described the copious fruit, rice, cereal, sesame, millet, wheat, grains and barley that gave the local people produce in excess of their needs, and which they could trade.[28] The Gangetic plain became the center of Indic civilization; we hear little about other parts of the subcontinent during Gotama's lifetime. Six great cities became centers of trade and industry: Sāvatthī, Saketā, Kosambī, Vārānasī, Rājagaha and Champā, and were linked by new trade routes. The cities were exciting places: their streets were crowded with brilliantly painted carriages, huge elephants carried merchandise to and from distant lands, and there was gambling, theater, dancing, prostitution and a rowdy tavern life, much of which shocked the people of the nearby villages. Merchants from all parts of India and from all castes mingled in the marketplace, and there was lively discussion of the new philosophical ideas in the streets, the city hall and the luxurious parks in the suburbs. The cities were dominated by the new men – merchants, businessmen and bankers – who no longer fit easily into the old caste system and were beginning to challenge the *brahmins* and *ksatriyas.*[29] This was all disturbing but invigorating. Urban dwellers felt at the cutting edge of change.

The political life of the region had also been transformed. The Ganges basin had originally been ruled by a number of small kingdoms and by a few so-called republics which were really oligarchies, based on the institutions of the old clans and tribes. Gotama was born in Sakka, the most northerly of these republics, and his father Suddhodana would have been a member of the *sangha,* the regular Assembly of aristocrats which governed the Sakyan clansmen and their families. The Sakyans were notoriously proud and independent. Their territory was so remote that Āryan culture had never taken root there, and they had no caste system. But times were changing. Kapilavatthu, the capital of Sakka, was now an important trading post on one of the new mercantile routes. The outside world had begun to invade the republic, which was gradually being pulled into the mainstream.[30] Like the other republics of Malla, Koliya, Videha, Naya and Vajji to the east of the region, Sakka felt threatened by the two new monarchies of Kosala and Magadha, which were aggressively and inexorably bringing the weaker and more old-fashioned states of the Gangetic plain under their control.

Kosala and Magadha were far more efficiently run than the old republics, where there was constant infighting and civil strife. These modern kingdoms had streamlined bureaucracies and armies which professed allegiance to the king alone, instead of to the tribe as a whole. This meant that each king had a personal fighting machine at his disposal, which gave him the power to impose order on his domains and to conquer neighboring territory. These modern monarchs were also able to police the new trade routes efficiently, and this pleased the merchants on whom the economy of the kingdoms depended.[31] The region enjoyed a new stability, but at a cost. Many were disturbed by the violence and ruthlessness of the new society, where kings could force their will upon the people, where the economy was fueled by greed, and where bankers and merchants, locked in aggressive competition, preyed upon one another. The traditional values seemed to be crumbling, a familiar way of life was disappearing, and the order that was taking its place was frightening and alien. It was no wonder that so many people felt life was *dukkha,* a word usually translated as 'suffering,' but whose meaning is better conveyed by such terms as 'unsatisfactory,' 'flawed,' and 'awry.'

In this changing society, the ancient Āryan religion of the *brahmins* seemed increasingly out of place. The old rituals had suited a settled rural community, but were beginning to seem cumbersome and archaic in the more mobile world of the cities. Merchants were constantly on the road and could not keep the fires burning, nor could they observe the *uposatha* days. Since these new men fit less and less easily into the caste system, many of them felt that they had been pushed into a spiritual vacuum. Animal sacrifice had made sense when stockbreeding had been the basis of the economy, but the new kingdoms depended upon agricultural crops. Cattle were becoming scarce and sacrifice seemed wasteful and cruel – too reminiscent of the violence that now characterized so much of public life. At a time when the urban communities were dominated by self-made men who had to rely on themselves, people increasingly resented the dominance of the *brahmins* and wanted to control their own spiritual destiny. Moreover, the sacrifices did not work. The *brahmins* alleged that these ritual actions (*kamma*) would bring the people riches and material success in this world, but these promised benefits usually failed to materialize. In the new economic climate, people in the cities wanted to concentrate on *kamma* which would yield a sounder investment.

The modern monarchies and the cities, dominated by a market economy, had made the peoples of the Gangetic region highly conscious of the rate of change. Urban dwellers could see for themselves that their society was being rapidly transformed; they could measure its progress and were experiencing a lifestyle that was very different from the repetitive rhythms of a rural community, which was based on the seasons and where everybody did the same things year after year. In the towns, people were beginning to realize that their actions (*kamma*) had long-term consequences, which they themselves might not experience but which they could see would affect future generations. The doctrine of reincarnation, which was of quite recent origin, suited this world much better than did the old Vedic faith. The theory of *kamma* stated that we had nobody to blame for our fate but ourselves and that our actions would reverberate in the very distant future. True, *kamma* could not release human beings from the wearisome round of *saṃsāra,* but good *kamma* would yield a valuable return since it ensured a more enjoyable existence next time. A few generations earlier, the doctrine of reincarnation had been a highly controversial one, known only to an elite few. But by Gotama's time, when people had become conscious of cause and effect in an entirely new way, everybody believed in it – even the *brahmins* themselves.[32]

But as in the other Axial countries, the people of northern India had begun to experiment with other religious ideas and practices which seemed to speak more directly to their altered conditions. Shortly before Gotama's birth, a circle of sages in the regions to the west of the Gangetic plain staged a secret rebellion against the old Vedic faith. They began to create a series of texts which were passed secretly from master to pupil. These new scriptures were called the *Upaniṣads,* a title which stressed the esoteric nature of this revolutionary lore, since it derived from the Sanskrit *apa-ni-sad* (to sit near). The *Upaniṣads* ostensibly relied upon the old Vedas, but reinterpreted them, giving them a more spiritual and interiorized significance; this marked the beginning of the tradition now known as Hinduism, another of the great religions formed during the Axial Age. The goal of the sages' spiritual quest was the absolute reality of *brahman,* the impersonal essence of the universe and the source of everything that exists. But *brahman* was not simply a remote and transcendent reality; it was also an immanent presence which pervaded everything that lived and breathed. In fact, by dint of the Upaniṣadic disciplines, a practitioner would find that *brahman* was present in the core of his own being. Salvation lay not in animal sacrifice, as the *brahmins* had taught, but in the spiritual realization that *brahman,* the absolute, eternal reality that is higher even than the gods, was identical to one's own deepest Self (*ātman*).[33]

The idea of an eternal and absolute Self would greatly exercise Gotama, as we shall see. It was a remarkable insight. To believe that one's innermost Self was identical with *brahman,* the supreme reality, was a startling act of faith in the sacred potential of humanity. The classic expression of this doctrine is found in the early *Chandogya Upaniṣad.* The *brahmin* Uddalaka wanted to show his son Svetaketu, who prided himself on his knowledge of the Vedas, the limitations of the old religion. He asked Svetaketu to dissolve a lump of salt in a beaker of water. The next morning, the salt had apparently vanished, but, of course, when Svetaketu sipped the water he found that the salt permeated the whole beakerful of liquid, even though it could not be seen. This was just like *brahman,* Uddalaka explained; you could not see It but nevertheless It was there. 'The whole universe has this first essence (*brahman*) as its Self (*ātman*). That is what the Self is; that is what *you* are, Svetaketu!'[34] This was rebellious indeed; once you understood that the Absolute was in everything, including yourself, there was no need for a priestly elite. People could find the ultimate for themselves, without cruel, pointless sacrifices, within their own being.

But the sages of the *Upaniṣads* were not alone in the rejection of the old faith of the *brahmins.* In the eastern part of the Gangetic region, most of the monks and ascetics who lived in the forest were unfamiliar with the spirituality of the *Upaniṣads,* which was still an underground, esoteric faith centered in the western plains. Some of the new ideas had leaked through on a popular level, however. There was no talk in the eastern Ganges of *brahman,* which is never mentioned in the Buddhist scriptures, but a folk version of this supreme principle had become popular in the cult of the new god Brahma, who, it was said, dwelt in the highest heaven of all. Gotama does not seem to have heard of *brahman,* but he was aware of Brahma, who, as we shall see, played a role in Gotama's own personal drama.[35] When Gotama left Kapilavatthu, he headed for this eastern region, traveling throughout the rest of his life in the new kingdoms of Kosala and Magadha and in the old adjacent republics. Here the spiritual rejection of the ancient Āryan traditions took a more practical turn. People were less interested in metaphysical speculation about the nature of ultimate reality and more concerned with personal liberation.

The forest-monks may not have been conversant with the transcendent *brahman*, but they longed to know *ātman*, the absolute Self within, and were devising various ways of accessing this eternal, immanent principle. The doctrine of the Self was attractive because it meant that liberation from the suffering of life was clearly within reach and required no priestly intermediaries. It also suited the individualism of the new society and its cult of self-reliance. Once a monk had found his real Self, he would understand at a profound level that pain and death were not the last words about the human condition. But how could a monk find this Self and thus gain release from the endless cycle of *saṃsāra?* Even though the Self was said to be within each person, the monks had discovered that it was very difficult to find it.

The spirituality of the eastern Gangetic region was much more populist. In the west, the Upaniṣadic sages guarded their doctrines from the masses; in the east, these questions were eagerly debated by the people.[36] As we have seen, they did not see the mendicant monks as useless parasites but as heroic pioneers. They were also honored as rebels. Like the Upaniṣadic sages, the monks defiantly rejected the old Vedic faith. At the start of his quest, an aspirant went through a ceremony known as the *Pabbajjā* ('Going Forth'): he had become a person who had literally walked out of Āryan society. The ritual required that the renunciant remove all the external signs of his caste and throw the utensils used in sacrifice into the fire. Henceforth, he would be called a *Sannyāsin* ('Caster-Off'), and his yellow robe became the insignia of his rebellion. Finally, the new monk ritually and symbolically swallowed the sacred fire, as a way, perhaps, of declaring his choice of a more interior religion.[37] He had deliberately rejected his place in the old world by repudiating the life of the householder, which was the backbone of the system: the married man kept the economy going, produced the next generation, paid for the all-important sacrifices and took care of the political life of society. The monks, however, cast aside these duties and pursued a radical freedom. They had left behind the structured space of the home for the untamed forests; they were no longer subject to the constraints of caste, no longer debarred from any activity by the accident of their birth. Like the merchant, they were mobile and could roam the world at will, responsible to nobody but themselves. Like the merchants, therefore, they were the new men of the era, whose whole lifestyle expressed the heightened sense of individualism that characterized the period.

In leaving home, therefore, Gotama was not abjuring the modern world for a more traditional or even archaic lifestyle (as monks are often perceived to be doing today), but was in the vanguard of change. His family, however, could scarcely be expected to share this view. The republic of Sakka was so isolated that it was cut off from the developing society that was growing up in the Ganges plain below and, as we have seen, had not even assimilated the Vedic ethos. The new ideas would have seemed foreign to most of the Sakyan people. Nevertheless, news of the rebellion of the forest-monks had obviously reached the republic and stirred the young Gotama. As we have seen, the Pāli texts give us a very brief account of his decision to leave home, but there is another more detailed story of Gotama's Going Forth, which brings out the deeper significance of the Pabbajjā.[38] It is found only in the later extended biographies and commentaries, such as the *Nidāna Kathā,* which was probably written in the fifth century C.E. But even though we only find this tale in the later Buddhist writings, it could be just as old as the Pāli legends. Some scholars believe that these late, consecutive biographies were based on an old narrative that was composed at about the same time that the Pāli Canon took its final shape, some one hundred years after Gotama's death. The Pāli legends were certainly familiar with this story, but they attribute it not to Gotama but to his predecessor, the Buddha Vipassī, who had achieved enlightenment in a previous age.[39] So the tale is an archetype, applicable to all Buddhas. It does not attempt to challenge the Pāli version of Gotama's Going Forth, nor does it purport to be historically sound, in our sense. Instead, this overtly mythological story, with its divine interventions and magical occurrences, represents an alternative interpretation of the crucial event of the Pabbajjā. This is what all Buddhas – Gotama no less than Vipassī – have to do at the beginning of their quest; indeed, everybody who seeks enlightenment must go through this transformative experience when he or she embarks on the spiritual life. The story is almost a paradigm of Axial Age spirituality. It shows how a human being becomes fully conscious, in the way that the Axial sages demanded, of his or her predicament. It is only when people become aware of the inescapable reality of pain that they can begin to become fully human. The story in the *Nidāna Kathā* is symbolic and has universal impact, because unawakened men and women all try to deny the suffering of life and pretend that it has nothing to do with them. Such denial is not only futile (because nobody is immune to pain and these facts of life will always break in), but also dangerous, because it imprisons people in a delusion that precludes spiritual development.

Thus the *Nidāna Kathā* tells us that when little Siddhattha was five days old, his father Suddhodana invited a hundred *brahmins* to a feast, so that they could examine the baby's body for marks which would foretell his future. Eight of the *brahmins* concluded that the child had a glorious future: he would either become a Buddha, who achieved the supreme spiritual enlightenment, or a Universal King, a hero of popular legend, who, it was said, would rule the whole world. He would possess a special divine chariot; each one of its four wheels rolled in the direction of one of the four quarters of the earth. This World Emperor would walk through the heavens with a massive retinue of soldiers, and would 'turn the Wheel of Righteousness,' establishing justice and right-living throughout the cosmos. This myth was clearly influenced by the new cult of kingship in the monarchies of Kosala and Magadha. Throughout Gotama's life, he had to confront this alternative destiny. The image of the Universal Monarch (*cakkavatti*) would become his symbolic alter ego, the opposite of everything that he did finally achieve. The *cakkavatti* might be powerful and his reign could even be beneficial to the world, but he is not a spiritually enlightened man, since his career depends entirely upon force. One of the *brahmins*, whose name was Kondañña, was convinced that little Siddhatta would never become a *cakkavatti*. Instead, he would renounce the comfortable life of the householder and become a Buddha who would overcome the ignorance and folly of the world.[40]

Suddhodana was not happy about this prophecy. He was determined that his son become a *cakkavatti*, which seemed to him a much more desirable option than the life of a world-renouncing ascetic. Kondañña had told him that one day Siddhatta would see four things – an old man, a sick person, a corpse and a monk – which would convince him to leave home and 'Go Forth.' Suddhodana, therefore, decided to shield his son from these disturbing sights: guards were posted around the palace to keep all upsetting reality at bay, and the boy became a virtual prisoner, even though he lived in luxury and had an apparently happy life. Gotama's pleasure-palace is a striking image of a mind in denial. As long as we persist in closing our minds and hearts to the universal pain, which surrounds us on all sides, we remain locked in an undeveloped version of ourselves, incapable of growth and spiritual insight. The young Siddhatta was living in a delusion, since his vision of the world did not coincide with the way things really were. Suddhodana is an example of exactly the kind of authority figure that later Buddhist tradition would condemn. He forced his own view upon his son and refused to let him make up his own mind. This type of coercion could only impede enlightenment, since it traps a person in a self which is inauthentic and in an infantile, unawakened state.

The gods, however, decided to intervene. They knew that even though his father refused to accept it, Gotama was a Bodhisatta, a man who was destined to become a Buddha. The gods could not themselves lead Gotama to enlightenment, of course, since they were also caught up in *saṃsāra* and needed a Buddha to teach them the way to find release as acutely as any human being. But the gods could give the Bodhisatta a much-needed nudge. When he had reached the age of twenty-nine, they decided that he had lived in this fool's paradise long enough, so they sent into the pleasure-park one of their own number, disguised as a senile old man, who was able to use his divine powers to elude Suddhodana's guards. When Gotama saw this old man, while driving in the park, he was horrified and had to ask Channa, the charioteer, what had happened to the man. Channa explained that he was simply old: everybody who lived long enough went into a similar decline. Gotama returned to the palace in a state of deep distress.

When he heard what had happened, Suddhodana redoubled the guard and tried to distract his son with new pleasures – but to no avail. On two further occasions, gods appeared to Gotama in the guise of a sick man and a corpse. Finally, Gotama and Channa drove past a god dressed in the yellow robe of a monk. Inspired by the gods, Channa told Gotama that this was a man who had renounced the world, and he praised the ascetic life so passionately that Gotama returned home in a very thoughtful mood. That night, he woke to find that the minstrels and dancers who had been entertaining him that evening had fallen asleep. All around his couch, beautiful women lay in disarray: 'Some with their bodies slick with phlegm and spittle; others were grinding their teeth, and muttering and talking incoherently in their sleep; others lay with their mouths wide open.' A shift had occurred in Gotama's view of the world. Now that he was aware of the suffering that lay in wait for every single being without exception, everything seemed ugly – even repellent. The veil that had concealed life's pain had been torn aside and the universe seemed a prison of pain and pointlessness. 'How oppressive and stifling it is!' Gotama exclaimed. He leapt out of bed and resolved to 'Go Forth' that very night.[41]

It is always tempting to try to shut out the suffering that is an inescapable part of the human condition, but once it has broken through the cautionary barricades we have erected against it, we can never see the world in the same way again. Life seems meaningless, and an Axial Age pioneer will feel compelled to break out of the old accepted patterns and try to find a new way of coping with this pain. Only when he had found an inner haven of peace would life seem meaningful and valuable once more. Gotama had permitted the spectacle of *dukkha* to invade his life and to tear his world apart. He had smashed the hard carapace in which so many of us encase ourselves in order to keep sorrow at a distance. But once he had let suffering in, his quest could begin. Before leaving home, he crept upstairs to take one last look at his sleeping wife and their baby, but could not bring himself to say goodbye. Then he stole out of the palace. He saddled his horse Kanthaka and rode through the city, with Channa clinging to the horse's tail in a desperate attempt to prevent his departure. The gods opened the city gates to let him out, and once he was outside Kapilavatthu, Gotama shaved his head and put on the yellow robe. Then he sent Channa and Kanthaka back to his father's house, and, we are told in another Buddhist legend, the horse died of a broken heart, but was reborn in one of the heavens of the cosmos as a god, as a reward for his part in the Buddha's enlightenment.

Before he could begin his quest in earnest, Gotama had to undergo one last temptation. Suddenly, Māra, the Lord of this world, the god of sin, greed and death, erupted threateningly before him. 'Don't become a monk! Don't renounce the world!' Māra begged. If Gotama would stay at home for just one more week, he would become a *cakkavatti* and rule the whole world. Think what good he could do! He could end life's suffering with his benevolent government. This was, however, the easy option and a delusion, because pain can never be conquered by force. It was the suggestion of an unenlightened being, and throughout Gotama's life, Māra would try to impede his progress and tempt him to lower his standards. That night, Gotama was easily able to ignore Māra's suggestion, but the angry god refused to give up. 'I will catch you,' he whispered to himself, 'the very first time you have a greedy, spiteful or unkind thought.' He followed Gotama around 'like an ever-present shadow,' to trap him in a moment of weakness.[42] Long after Gotama had attained the supreme enlightenment, he still had to be on his guard against Māra, who represents what Jungian psychologists would, perhaps, call his shadow-side, all the unconscious elements within the psyche which fight against our liberation. Enlightenment is never easy. It is frightening to leave our old selves behind, because they are the only way we know how to live. Even if the familiar is unsatisfactory, we tend to cling to it because we are afraid of the unknown. But the holy life that Gotama had undertaken demanded that he leave behind everything he loved and everything that made up his unregenerate personality. At every turn, he had to contend with that part of himself (symbolized by Māra) which shrank from this total self-abandonment. Gotama was looking for a wholly different way of living as a human being, and to bring this new self to birth would demand a long, difficult labor. It would also demand skill, and Gotama set off to find a teacher who could instruct him in the path to Enlightenment.

2 QUEST

ONCE GOTAMA HAD left the remote republic of Sakka behind and entered the Kingdom of Magadha, he had arrived at the heart of the new civilization. First, the Pāli legend tells us, he stayed for a while outside Rājagaha, the capital of Magadha and one of the most powerful of the developing cities. While begging for his food, he is said to have come to the attention of no less a person than King Bimbisāra himself, who was so impressed by the young Sakyan *bhikkhu* that he wanted to make him his heir.[1] This is clearly a fictional embellishment of Gotama's first visit to Rājagaha, but the incident highlights an important aspect of his future mission. Gotama had belonged to one of the leading families in Kapilavatthu and felt quite at ease with kings and aristocrats. There had been no caste system in Sakka, but once he arrived in the mainstream society of the region, he presented himself as a *ksatriya,* a member of the caste responsible for government. But Gotama was able to look at the structures of Vedic society with the objectivity of an outsider. He had not been brought up to revere the *brahmins* and never felt at a disadvantage with them; later, when he founded his Order, he rejected any rigid categorization on grounds of heredity. This critical stance would stand him in good stead in the cities, where the caste system was disintegrating. It is also significant that Gotama's first port of call was not a remote hermitage but a big industrial city. He would spend most of his working life in the towns and cities of the Ganges, where there was widespread malaise and bewilderment resulting from the change and upheaval that urbanization brought with it, and where consequently there was much spiritual hunger.

Gotama did not spend long in Rājagaha on this first visit, but set off in search of a teacher who could guide him through his spiritual apprenticeship and teach him the rudiments of the holy life. In Sakka, Gotama had probably seen very few monks, but as soon as he started to travel along the new trade routes that linked the cities of the region, he would have been struck by the large crowds of wandering *bhikkhus* in their yellow robes, carrying their begging bowls and walking beside the merchants. In the towns, he would have watched them standing silently in the doorways of the houses, not asking for food directly but simply holding out their bowls, which the householders, anxious to acquire merit that would earn them a good rebirth, were usually glad to fill with leftovers. When Gotama left the road to sleep in the forests of banyan, ebony and palm trees that skirted the cultivated land, he would have come across bands of monks living together in encampments. Some of them had brought their wives along and had set up a household in the wild, while they pursued the holy life. There were even some *brahmins* who had undertaken the 'noble quest,' still tending the three sacred fires and seeking enlightenment in a more strictly Vedic context. During the monsoon rains, which hit the region in mid-June and lasted well into September, travel became impossible, and many of the monks used to live together in the forests or in the suburban parks and cemeteries until the floods subsided and the roads became passable again. By the time Gotama came to join them, the wandering *bhikkhus* were a notable feature of the landscape and a force to be reckoned with in society. Like the merchants, they had almost become a fifth caste.[2]

In the early days, many had adopted this special *ājīva* vocation mainly to escape from the drudgery of domesticity and a regular job. There were always some renouncers who were chiefly dropouts, debtors, bankrupts and fugitives from justice. But by the time Gotama embarked on his quest, they were becoming more organized and even the most uncommitted monks had to profess an ideology that justified their existence. Hence a number of different schools had developed. In the efficient new kingdoms of Kosala and Magadha, the government had begun to exercise more control over the inhabitants and would not allow people to embrace an alternative lifestyle that made no contribution to society as a whole. The monks had to prove that they were not parasites, but philosophers whose beliefs could improve the spiritual health of the country.[3]

Most of the new ideologies centered on the doctrine of reincarnation and *kamma:* their object was to gain liberation from the ceaseless round of *saṃsāra* that propelled them from one existence to another. The *Upaniṣads* had taught that the chief cause of suffering was ignorance: once a seeker had acquired a deep knowledge of his true and absolute Self (*ātman*), he would find that he no longer experienced pain so acutely and would have intimations of a final release. But the monks of Magadha, Kosala and the republics to the east of the Gangetic plain were more interested in practicalities. Instead of regarding ignorance as the chief cause of *dukkha,* they saw desire (*tanhā*) as the chief culprit. By desire they did not mean those noble yearnings that inspired human beings to such inspiring and elevating pursuits as the holy life, but the type of craving that makes us say 'I want.' They were very worried by the greed and egotism of the new society. They were, as we have seen, men of their time and had imbibed the ethos of individualism and self-reliance that was emerging in the marketplace, but, like the other sages of the Axial Age, they knew that egotism could be dangerous. The monks of the eastern Ganges were convinced that it was this thirsty *tanhā* that kept people bound to *saṃsāra*. They reasoned that all our actions were, to an extent, inspired by desire. When we found that we wanted something, we took steps to get it; when a man lusted for a woman, he took the trouble to seduce her; when people fell in love, they wanted to possess the beloved and clung and yearned compulsively. Nobody would bother to do an arduous and frequently boring job in order to earn a living unless he or she wanted material comforts. So desire fueled people's actions (*kamma*), but every single action had long-term consequences and conditioned the kind of existence the person would have in his or her next life.

It followed that *kamma* led to rebirth; if we could avoid performing any actions at all, we might have a chance of liberating ourselves from the cycle of new birth, suffering and redeath. But our desires impelled us to act, so, the monks concluded, if we could eliminate *tanhā* from our hearts and minds, we would perform fewer *kamma*. But a householder had no chance of ridding himself of desire. His whole life consisted of one doomed activity after another.[4] It was his duty as a married man to beget offspring, and without some degree of lust, he would not be able to sleep with his wife.

Unless he felt a modicum of greed, he could not engage in trade or industry with any success or conviction. If he was a king or a *ksatriya,* he would be quite unable to govern or wage war against his enemies if he had no desire for power. Indeed, without *tanhā* and the actions (*kamma*) that resulted from it, society would come to a halt. A householder's life, dominated as it was by lust, greed and ambition, compelled him to activities that bound him to the web of existence: inevitably, he would be born again to endure another life of pain. True, a householder could acquire merit by performing good *kamma.* He could give alms to a *bhikkhu,* for example, and thus build up a reserve of credit that could benefit him in the future. But because all *kamma* were limited, they could only have finite consequences. They could not bring the householder to the immeasurable peace of Nibbāṇa. The best that our *kamma* could do for us was to ensure that in the next life we might be reborn as a god in one of the heavenly worlds, but even that celestial existence would come to an end one day. Consequently, the endless round of duties and responsibilities that made up a householder's life became a symbol of *saṃsāra* and of exclusion from holiness. Tied to this treadmill of fateful activity, the householder had no hope of liberation.

But the monk was in a better position. He had given up sex; he had no children or dependents to support, and need not do a job or engage in trade. Compared with the householder, he enjoyed a relatively action-free life.[5] But even though he performed fewer *kamma,* the monk still experienced desires which tied him to this life. Even the most committed monk knew that he had not liberated himself from craving. He was still afflicted by lust, and still yearned occasionally for a little comfort in his life. Indeed, deprivation sometimes increased desire. How could a monk liberate himself? How could he gain access to his true Self and free it from the material world, when, despite his best endeavors, he still found himself hankering for earthly things? A number of different solutions emerged in the main monastic schools. A teacher developed a *dhamma,* a system of doctrine and discipline, which, he believed, would deal with these intractable difficulties. He then gathered a group of disciples, and formed what was known as a *sangha* or *gana* (old Vedic terms for tribal groupings in the region). These *sanghas* were not tightly knit bodies, like modern religious orders. They had little or no common life, no formal rule of conduct, and members came and went as they chose. There was nothing to stop a monk from dropping his teacher as soon as he found a more congenial *dhamma,* and the monks seemed to shop around to find the best teacher they could. It became customary for the *bhikkhus* to hail one another on the road, asking: 'Who is your teacher? And which *dhamma* do you follow?'

As Gotama traveled through Magadha and Kosala, he himself would probably have called out to passing monks in this way, because he was looking for a teacher and a *sangha.* Initially, he might have found the clash of ideologies confusing. The *sanghas* were competitive and promoted their *dhammas* as aggressively as merchants pushed their wares in the marketplace. Zealous disciples may well have called their teachers 'Buddhas' ('Enlightened Ones') or 'Teacher of Gods and Men.'[6] As in the other Axial countries, there was a ferment of debate, much sophisticated argument and a great deal of public interest in the issues. The religious life was not the preserve of a few eccentric fanatics, but was a matter of concern to everybody. Teachers debated with one another in the city halls; crowds would gather to hear a public sermon.[7] Lay people took sides, supporting one *sangha* against the others. When the leader of one of the *sanghas* arrived in town, householders, merchants and government officials would seek him out, interrogate him about his *dhamma,* and discuss its merits with the same kind of enthusiasm with which people discuss football teams today. The laity could appreciate the finer points in these debates, but their interest was never theoretical. Religious knowledge in India had one criterion: did it work? Would it transform an individual, mitigate the pain of life, bring peace and hope of a final release? Nobody was interested in metaphysical doctrine for its own sake. A *dhamma* had to have a practical orientation; nearly all the ideologies of the forest-monks, for example, tried to mitigate the aggression of the new society, promoting the ethic of *ahiṃsā* (harmlessness), which advocated gentleness and affability.

Thus the Ājīvakas, who followed the teachers Makkali Gosāla and Pūraṇa Kassapa, denied the current theory of *kamma:* they believed that everybody would eventually enjoy liberation from *saṃsāra,* even though this process could take thousands of years. Each person had to pass through a fixed number of lives and experience every form of life. The point of this *dhamma* was to cultivate peace of mind; there was no point in worrying about the future, since everything was predestined. In a similar spirit, the Materialists, led by the sage Ajita, denied the doctrine of reincarnation, arguing that since human beings were wholly physical creatures, they would simply return to the elements after death. The way you behaved was a matter of no importance, therefore, since everybody had the same fate; but it was probably better to foster goodwill and happiness by doing as one pleased and performing only those *kamma* which furthered those ends. Sañjaya, the leader of the Skeptics, rejected the possibility of any final truth and taught that all *kamma* should aim at cultivating friendship and peace of mind. Since all truth was relative, discussion could lead only to acrimony and should be avoided. The Jains, led in Gotama's lifetime by Vardhamāna Jnātrputra, known as Mahāvīra (the Great Hero), believed that bad *kamma* covered the soul with a fine dust, which weighed it down. Some, therefore, tried to avoid any activity whatsoever, especially those *kamma* which might injure another creature – even a plant or an insect. Some Jains tried to remain immobile, lest they inadvertently tread on a stick or spill a drop of water, since these lower forms of life all contained living souls, trapped by bad *kamma* performed in previous lives. But Jains often combined this extraordinary gentleness with a violence toward themselves, doing horrific penance in an attempt to burn away the effects of bad *kamma:* they would starve themselves, refuse to drink or to wash, and expose themselves to the extremes of heat and cold.[8]

Gotama did not join any of these *sanghas.* Instead he went to the neighborhood of Vesālī, the capital of the Videha republic, to be initiated in the *dhamma* of Ālāra Kālāma, who seems to have taught a form of Sāṃkhya.[9] Gotama may have already been familiar with this school, since the philosophy of Sāṃkhya (discrimination) had first been taught by the seventh-century teacher Kapila, who had links with Kapilavatthu. This school believed that ignorance, rather than desire, lay at the root of our problems; our suffering derived from our lack of understanding of the true Self. We confused this Self with our ordinary psychomental life, but to gain liberation we had to become aware at a profound level that the Self had nothing to do with these transient, limited and unsatisfactory states of mind. The Self was eternal and identical with the Absolute Spirit (*puruṣa*) that is dormant in every thing and every body but concealed by the material world of nature (*praktṛi*). The goal of the holy life, according to Sāṃkhya, was to learn to discriminate *puruṣa* from *praktṛi*. The aspirant had to learn to live above the confusion of the emotions and cultivate the intellect, the purest part of the human being, which had the power to reflect the eternal Spirit, in the same way that a flower is reflected in a mirror. This was not an easy process, but as soon as a monk became truly aware that his true Self was entirely free, absolute and eternal, he achieved liberation. Nature (*praktṛi*) would then immediately withdraw from the Self, 'like a dancer who departs after having satisfied her master's desire,' as one of the classic texts puts it.[10] Once this had happened, the monk would achieve enlightenment, because he had woken up to his true nature. Suffering could no longer touch him, because he knew that he was eternal and absolute. Indeed, he would find himself saying 'it suffers' rather than 'I suffer,' because pain had become a remote experience, distant from what he now understood to be his truest identity. The enlightened sage would continue to live in the world and would burn up the remains of the bad *kamma* he had committed, but when he died he would never be reborn, because he had achieved emancipation from material *praktṛi*.[11]

Gotama found Sāṃkhya congenial and, when he came to formulate his own *dhamma*, he retained some elements of this philosophy. It was clearly an attractive ideology to somebody like Gotama, who had so recently experienced the disenchantment of the world, because it taught the aspirant to look for holiness everywhere. Nature (*praktṛi*) was simply an ephemeral phenomenon, and however disturbing it appeared, it was not the final reality. To those who felt that the world had become an alien place, however, Sāṃkhya was a healing vision, because it taught that, despite its unpromising exterior, nature was our friend. It could help human beings to achieve enlightenment. Like men and women, every single creature in the natural world was also driven by the need to liberate the Self; Nature was thus bent on superseding itself and allowing the Self to go free. Even suffering had a redemptive role, because the more we suffered, the more we longed for an existence that would be free of such pain; the more we experienced the constraints of the world of *praktṛi*, the more we yearned for release. The more fully we realized that our lives were conditioned by outside forces, the more we desired the absolute, unconditioned reality of *puruṣa*. But however strong his desire, an ascetic often found that it was extremely difficult to liberate himself from the material world. How could mortal human beings, plagued by the turbulent life of the emotions and the anarchic life of the body, rise above this disturbance and live by the intellect alone?

Gotama soon came up against this problem and found that contemplating the truths of Sāṃkhya brought no real relief, but at first he made great strides. Ālāra Kālāma accepted him as a pupil and promised him that in a very short time he would understand the *dhamma* and know as much as his teacher. He would make the doctrine his own. Gotama quickly mastered the essentials, and was soon able to recite the teachings of his master as proficiently as could the other members of the *sangha*, but he was not convinced. Something was missing. Ālāra Kālāma had assured him that he would 'realize' these teachings and achieve a 'direct knowledge' of them. They would not remain truths that existed apart from himself, but would be so integrated with his own psyche that they would become a reality in his life. Soon he would become a living embodiment of the *dhamma.* But this was not happening. He was not 'entering into' the doctrine and 'dwelling in it,' as Ālāra Kālāma had predicted; the teachings remained remote, metaphysical abstractions and seemed to have little to do with him personally. Try as he would, he could gain no glimmer of his real Self, which remained obstinately hidden by what seemed an impenetrable rind of *prakṛti.* This is a common religious predicament. People often take the truths of a tradition on faith, accepting the testimony of other people, but find that the inner kernel of the religion, its luminous essence, remains elusive. But Gotama had little time for this approach. He always refused to take anything on trust, and later, when he had his own *sangha,* he insistently warned his disciples not to take anything at all on hearsay. They must not swallow everything that their teacher told them uncritically, but test the *dhamma* at every point, making sure that it resonated with their own experience.

So even at this very early stage in his quest, he refused to accept Ālāra Kālāma's *dhamma* as a matter of faith. He went to his master and asked him how he had managed to 'realize' these doctrines: Surely he had not simply taken somebody else's word for all this? Ālāra Kālāma admitted that he had not achieved his 'direct knowledge' of Sāṃkhya by contemplation alone. He had not penetrated these doctrines simply by normal, rational thought, but by using the disciplines of yoga.[12]

We do not know when the yogic exercises were first evolved in India.[13] There is evidence that some form of yoga might have been practiced in the subcontinent before the invasion of the Āryan tribes. Seals have been found dating from the second millennium B.C.E. which show figures sitting in what might be a yogic position. There is no written account of yoga until long after Gotama's lifetime. The classical texts were composed in the second or third century C.E. and based on the teachings of a mystic called Patañjali, who lived in the second century B.C.E. Patañjali's methods of contemplation and concentration were based on the philosophy of Sāṃkhya but started at the point where Sāṃkhya breaks off. His aim was not to propound a metaphysical theory but to cultivate a different mode of consciousness which can truly enter into truths which lie beyond the reach of the senses. This involves the suppression of normal consciousness, by means of exacting psychological and physiological techniques which give the yogin insights that are suprasensory and extrarational. Like Ālāra Kālāma, Patañjali knew that ordinary speculation and meditation could not liberate the Self from *praktṛi:* the yogin had to achieve this by sheer force. He had to abolish his ordinary ways of perceiving reality, cancel out his normal thought processes, get rid of his mundane (lower-case) self, and, as it were, bludgeon his unwilling, recalcitrant mind to a state that lay beyond the reach of error and illusion. Again, there was nothing supernatural about yoga. Patañjali believed that the yogin was simply exploiting his natural psychological and mental capacities. Even though Patañjali was teaching long after the Buddha's death, it seems clear that the practice of yoga, often linked with Sāṃkhya, was well established in the Ganges region during Gotama's lifetime and was popular among the forest-monks. Yoga proved to be crucial to Gotama's enlightenment and he would adapt its traditional disciplines to develop his own *dhamma.* It is, therefore, important to understand the traditional yogic methods, which Gotama probably learned from Ālāra Kālāma and which put him onto the road to Nibbāṇa.

The word 'yoga' derives from the verb *yuj:* 'to yoke' or 'to bind together.'[14] Its goal was to link the mind of the yogin with his Self and to tether all the powers and impulses of the mind, so that consciousness becomes unified in a way that is normally impossible for human beings. Our minds are easily distracted. It is often hard to concentrate on one thing for a long time. Thoughts and fantasies seem to rise unbidden to the surface of the mind, even at the most inappropriate moments. We appear to have little control over these unconscious impulses. A great deal of our mental activity is automatic: one image summons up another, forged together by associations that have long been forgotten and have retreated into oblivion. We rarely consider an object or an idea as it is in itself, because it comes saturated with personal associations that immediately distort it and make it impossible for us to consider it objectively. Some of these psychomental processes are filled with pain: they are characterized by ignorance, egotism, passion, disgust and an instinct for self-preservation. They are powerful because they are rooted in the subconscious activities (*vāsanās*) that are difficult to control but that have a profound effect on our behavior. Long before Freud and Jung developed modern psychoanalysis, the yogins of India had discovered the unconscious mind and had, to a degree, learned to master it. Yoga was thus deeply in line with the Axial Age ethos – its attempt to make human beings more fully conscious of themselves and bring what had only been dimly intuited into the clear light of day. It enabled the practitioner to recognize these unruly *vāsanās* and get rid of them, if they impeded his spiritual progress. This was a difficult process, and the yogin needed careful supervision at each step of the way by a teacher, just as the modern analysand needs the support of his or her analyst. To achieve this control of the unconscious, the yogin had to break all ties with the normal world. First, like any monk, he had to 'Go Forth,' leaving society behind. Then he had to undergo an exacting regimen which took him, step by step, beyond ordinary behavior-patterns and habits of mind. He would, as it were, put his old self to death and, it was hoped, thus awaken his true Self, an entirely different mode of being.

All this will sound strange to some Western people who have had a very different experience of yoga. The sages and prophets of the Axial Age were gradually realizing that egotism was the greatest hindrance to an experience of the absolute and sacred reality they sought. A man or a woman had to lay aside the selfishness that seems so endemic to our humanity if he or she wished to apprehend the reality of God, *brahman* or Nibbāṇa. The Chinese philosophers taught that people must submit their desires and behavior to the essential rhythms of life if they wanted to achieve enlightenment. The Hebrew prophets spoke of submission to the will of God. Later, Jesus would tell his disciples that the spiritual quest demanded a death to self: a grain of wheat had to fall into the ground and die before it attained its full potential and bore fruit. Muhammad would preach the importance of *islām,* an existential surrender of the entire being to God. The abandonment of selfishness and egotism would, as we shall see, become the linchpin of Gotama's own *dhamma,* but the yogins of India had already appreciated the importance of this. Yoga can be described as the systematic dismantling of the egotism which distorts our view of the world and impedes our spiritual progress. Those who practice yoga in America and Europe today do not always have this objective. They often use the disciplines of yoga to improve their health. These exercises of concentration have been found to help people to relax or suppress excessive anxiety. Sometimes the techniques of visualization used by yogins to achieve spiritual ecstasy are employed by cancer sufferers: they try to imagine the diseased cells and to evoke subconscious forces to combat the progress of the illness. Certainly, the yogic exercises can enhance our control and induce a serenity if properly practiced, but the original yogins did not embark on this path in order to feel better and to live a more normal life. They wanted to abolish normality and wipe out their mundane selves.

Many of the monks of the Ganges plain had realized, as Gotama did, that they could not achieve the liberation they sought by contemplating a *dhamma* in a logical, discursive way. This rational manner of thinking employed only a small part of the mind, which, once they tried to focus exclusively on spiritual matters, proved to have an anarchic life of its own. They found that they were constantly struggling with a host of distractions and unhelpful associations that invaded their consciousness, however hard they tried to concentrate. Once they began to put the teachings of a *dhamma* into practicc, they also discovered all kinds of resistance within themselves which seemed beyond their control. Some buried part of themselves still longed for forbidden things, however great their willpower. It seemed that there were latent tendencies in the psyche which fought perversely against enlightenment, forces which the Buddhist texts personify in the figure of Māra. Often these subconscious impulses were the result of past conditioning, implanted within the monks before they had attained the age of reason, or part of their genetic inheritance. The Ganges monks did not talk about genes, of course; they attributed this resistance to bad *kamma* in a previous life. But how could they get past this conditioning to the absolute Self, which, they were convinced, lay beyond this mental turmoil? How could they rescue the Self from this frenzied *praktṛi?*

The monks sought a freedom that is impossible for a normal consciousness and that is far more radical than the liberty pursued today in the West, which usually demands that we learn to come to terms with our limitations. The monks of India wanted to break free of the conditioning that characterized the human personality, and to cancel out the constraints of time and place that limit our perception. The freedom they sought was probably close to what St. Paul would later call 'the freedom of the sons of God,"[15] but they were not content to wait to experience this in the heavenly world. They would achieve it by their own efforts here and now. The disciplines of yoga were designed to destroy the unconscious impediments to enlightenment and to decondition the human personality. Once that had been done, the yogins believed that they would at last become one with their true Self, which was Unconditioned, Eternal and Absolute.

The Self was, therefore, the chief symbol of the sacred dimension of existence, performing the same function as God in monotheism, as *brahman/ātman* in Hinduism, and as the Good in Platonic philosophy. When Gotama had tried to 'dwell' in Ālāra Kālāma's *dhamma,* he had wanted to enter into and inhabit the type of peace and wholeness that, according to the book of Genesis, the first human beings had experienced in Eden. It was not enough to know this Edenic peace, this *shalōm,* this Nibbāṇa notionally; he wanted the kind of 'direct knowledge' that would envelop him as completely as the physical atmosphere in which we live and breathe. He was convinced that he would discover this still sense of transcendent harmony in the depths of his psyche, and that it would transform him utterly: he would attain a new Self that was no longer vulnerable to the sufferings that flesh is heir to. In all the Axial countries, people were seeking more interior forms of spirituality, but few did this as thoroughly as the Indian yogins. One of the insights of the Axial Age was that the Sacred was not simply something that was 'out there;' it was also immanent and present in the ground of each person's being, a perception classically expressed in the Upaniṣadic vision of the identity of *brahman* and *ātman*. Yet even though the Sacred was as close to us as our own selves, it proved to be extremely hard to find. The gates of Eden had closed. In the old days, it was thought that the Sacred had been easily accessible to humanity. The ancient religions had believed that the deities, human beings and all natural phenomena had been composed of the same divine substance: there was no ontological gulf between humanity and the gods. But part of the distress that precipitated the Axial Age was that this sacred or divine dimension had somehow retreated from the world and become in some sense alien to men and women.

In the early texts of the Hebrew Bible, we read, for example, that Abraham had once shared a meal with his God, who had appeared in his encampment as an ordinary traveler.[16] But for the Axial Age prophets, God was often experienced as a devastating shock. Isaiah was filled with mortal terror when he had a vision of God in the Temple;[17] Jeremiah knew the divine as a pain that convulsed his limbs, broke his heart and made him stagger around like a drunk.[18] The whole career of Ezekiel, who may have been a contemporary of Gotama, illustrates the radical discontinuity that now existed between the Sacred on the one hand, and the conscious, self-protecting self, on the other: God afflicted the prophet with such anxiety that he could not stop trembling; when his wife died, God forbade him to mourn; God forced him to eat excrement and to walk around town with packed bags like a refugee.[19] Sometimes, in order to enter the divine presence, it seemed necessary to deny the normal responses of a civilized individual and to do violence to the mundane self. The early yogins were attempting the same kind of assault upon their ordinary consciousness in order to propel themselves into an apprehension of the Unconditioned and Absolute Self, which they believed to be within.

Yogins believed that the Self could only be liberated if they destroyed their normal thought processes, extinguished their thoughts and feelings, and wiped out the unconscious *vāsanās* that fought against enlightenment. They were engaged in a war against their conventional mental habits. At each point of his interior journey, the yogin did the opposite of what came naturally; each yogic discipline was crafted to undermine ordinary responses. Like any ascetic, the yogin began his spiritual life by 'Going Forth' from society, but he then went one step further. He would not even share the same psyche as a householder; he was 'Going Forth' from humanity itself. Instead of seeking fulfilment in the profane world, the yogins of India determined, at each step of their journey, that they would refuse to live in it.

Ālāra Kālāma would probably have initiated Gotama into these yogic exercises, one by one. But first, before Gotama could even begin to meditate, he had to lay a sound foundation of morality. Ethical disciplines would curb his egotism and purify his life, by paring it down to essentials. Yoga gives the practitioner a concentration and self-discipline so powerful that it could become demonic if used for selfish ends. Accordingly, the aspirant had to observe five 'prohibitions' (*yama*) to make sure that he had his recalcitrant (lower-case) self firmly under control. The *yama* forbade the aspirant to steal, lie, take intoxicants, kill or harm another creature, or to engage in sexual intercourse. These rules were similar to those prescribed for the lay disciples of the Jains, and reflect the ethic of *ahiṃsā* (harmlessness), and the determination to resist desire and to achieve absolute mental and physical clarity, which most of the Ganges ascetics had in common. Gotama would not have been permitted to proceed to the more advanced yogic disciplines until these *yama* had become second nature.[20] He also had to practice certain *niyamas* (bodily and psychic exercises), which included scrupulous cleanliness, the study of the *dhamma,* and the cultivation of an habitual serenity. In addition, there were ascetic practices (*tapas*): the aspirant had to put up with the extremes of heat and cold, hunger and thirst without complaint, and to control his words and gestures, which must never betray his inner thoughts. It was not an easy process, but once Gotama had mastered the *yama* and *niyamas,* he probably began to experience the 'indescribable happiness' that, the yogic classics tell us, is the result of this self-control, sobriety and *ahiṃsā.*[21]

Gotama was then ready for the first of the truly yogic disciplines: *āsana,* the physical posture that is characteristic of yoga.[22] Each one of these methods entailed a denial of a natural human tendency and demonstrated the yogin's principled refusal of the world. In *āsana,* he learned to cut the link between his mind and his senses by refusing to move. He had to sit with crossed legs and straight back in a completely motionless position. It would have made him realize that, left to themselves, our bodies are in constant motion: we blink, scratch, stretch, shift from one buttock to another, and turn our heads in response to stimulus. Even in sleep we are not really still. But in *āsana,* the yogin is so motionless that he seems more like a statue or a plant than a human being. Once mastered, however, the unnatural stillness mirrors the interior tranquility that he is trying to achieve.

Next, the yogin refuses to breathe. Respiration is probably the most fundamental, automatic and instinctive of our bodily functions and absolutely essential to life. We do not usually think about our breathing, but now Gotama would have had to master the art of *prāṇāyāma*, breathing progressively more and more slowly.[23] The ultimate goal was to pause for as long as possible between a gradual exhalation and inhalation, so that it seemed as though respiration had entirely ceased. *Prāṇāyāma* is very different from the arrhythmic breathing of ordinary life and more similar to the way we breathe during sleep, when the unconscious becomes more accessible to us in dreams and hypnogogic imagery. Not only did the refusal to breathe show the yogin's radical denial of the world; from the start, *prāṇāyāma* was found to have a profound effect on his mental state. In the early stages, aspirants still find that it brings on a sensation comparable to the effect of music, especially when played by oneself: there is a feeling of grandeur, expansiveness and calm nobility. It seems as though one is taking possession of one's own body.[24]

Once Gotama had mastered these physical disciplines, he was ready for the mental exercise of *ekāgratā:* concentration 'on a single point.'[25] In this, the yogin refused to think. Aspirants learned to focus on an object or an idea, to exclude any other emotion or association, and refused to entertain a single one of the distractions that rushed into their minds.

Gotama was gradually separating himself from normality and trying to approximate the autonomy of the eternal Self. He learned *pratyāhāra* (withdrawal of the senses), the ability to contemplate an object with the intellect alone, while his senses remained quiescent.[26] In *dhārāṇa* (concentration) he was taught to visualize the Self in the ground of his being, like a lotos rising from the pond or an inner light. During his meditation, by suspending his breathing, the aspirant hoped that he would become conscious of his own consciousness and penetrate to the heart of his intellect, where, it was thought, he would be able to see a reflection of the eternal Spirit (*puruṣa*).[27] Each *dhārāṇa* was supposed to last for twelve *prāṇāyāmas;* and after twelve *dhārāṇas* the yogin had sunk so deeply into himself that he spontaneously attained a state of 'trance' (*dhyāna;* in Pāli, *jhāna*).[28]

All this, the texts insist, is quite different from the reflections that we make in everyday life. Nor is it like a drug-induced state. Once a skilled yogin had mastered these disciplines, he usually found that he had achieved a new invulnerability, at least for the duration of his meditation. He no longer noticed the weather; the restless stream of his consciousness had been brought under control, and, like the Self, he had become impervious to the tensions and changes of his environment. He found that he became absorbed in the object or mental image he was contemplating in this way. Because he had suppressed his memory and the flood of undisciplined personal associations that an object usually evoked, he was no longer distracted from it to his own concerns, he did not subjectivize it, but could see it 'as it really was,' an important phrase for yogins. The 'I' was beginning to disappear from his thinking, and the object was no longer seen through the filter of his own experience. As a result, even the most humdrum of objects revealed wholly new qualities. Some aspirants might have imagined that at this point they were beginning to glimpse the *puruṣa* through the distorting film of *praktṛi.*

When, using these techniques, the yogin meditated on the doctrines of his *dhamma,* he experienced them so vividly that a rational formulation of these truths paled in comparison.

This was what Ālāra Kālāma had meant by 'direct' knowledge, since the delusions and egotism of normal consciousness no longer came between the yogin and his *dhamma;* he 'saw' it with new clarity, without the distorting film of subjective associations. These experiences are not delusions. The psychophysical changes wrought by *prāṇāyāma* and the disciplines that taught the yogin to manipulate his mental processes and even to monitor his unconscious impulses did bring about a change of consciousness. The skilled yogin could now perform mental feats that were impossible for a layman; he had revealed the way the mind could work when trained in a certain manner. New capacities had come to light as a result of his expertise, just as a dancer or an athlete displays the full abilities of the human body. Modern researchers have noted that during meditation, a yogin's heart rate slows down, his brain rhythms go into a different mode, he becomes detached neurologically from his surroundings and acutely sensitive to the object of his contemplation.[29]

Once he had entered his trance (*jhāna*), the yogin progressed through a series of increasingly deep mental states, which bear little relation to ordinary experience. In the first stage of *jhāna,* he would become entirely oblivious to the immediate environment, and feel a sensation of great joy and delight, which, a yogin could only assume, was the beginning of his final liberation. He still had occasional ideas, and isolated thoughts would flicker across his mind, but he found that for the duration of this trance he was beyond the reach of desire, pleasure or pain, and could gaze in rapt concentration on the object, symbol or doctrine that he was contemplating. In the second and third *jhānas,* the yogin had become so absorbed in these truths that he had entirely stopped thinking and was no longer even conscious of the pure happiness he had enjoyed a short while before. In the fourth and final *jhāna*, he had become so fused with the symbols of his *dhamma* that he felt he had become one with them, and was conscious of nothing else. There was nothing supernatural about these states. The yogin knew that he had created them for himself, but, not surprisingly, he did imagine that he was indeed leaving the world behind and drawing near to his goal. If he was really skilled, he could go beyond the *jhānas*, and enter a series of four *āyatanas* (meditative states) that were so intense that the early yogins felt that they had entered the realms inhabited by the gods.[30] The yogin experienced progressively four mental states that seemed to introduce him to new modes of being: a sense of infinity; a pure consciousness that is aware only of itself; and a perception of absence, which is, paradoxically, a plenitude. Only very gifted yogins reached this third *āyatana*, which was called 'Nothingness' because it bore no relation to any form of existence in profane experience. It was not another being. There were no words or concepts adequate to describe it. It was, therefore, more accurate to call it 'Nothing' than 'Something.' Some have described it as similar to walking into a room and finding nothing there: there was a sense of emptiness, space and freedom.

Monotheists have made similar remarks about their experience of God. Jewish, Christian and Muslim theologians have all, in different ways, called the most elevated emanations of the divine in human consciousness 'Nothing.' They have also said that it was better to say that God did not exist, because God was not simply another phenomenon. When confronted with transcendence or holiness, language stumbles under impossible difficulties, and this kind of negative terminology is one way that mystics instinctively adopt to emphasize its 'otherness.'[31] Understandably, those yogins who had reached these *āyatanas* imagined that they had finally experienced the illimitable Self that resided in the core of their being. Ālāra Kālāma was one of the few yogins of his day to have attained the plane of 'Nothingness'; he claimed that he had 'entered into' the Self which was the goal of his quest. Gotama was an incredibly gifted student. Yoga usually required a long apprenticeship that could last a lifetime, but in quite a short time, Gotama was able to tell his master that he had reached the plane of 'Nothingness' too. Ālāra Kālāma was delighted. He invited Gotama to become his partner in the leadership of the *sangha*, but Gotama refused. He also decided to leave Ālāra Kālāma's sect.

Gotama had no problem with the yogic method and would use it for the rest of his life. But he could not accept his master's interpretation of his meditative experience. Here he showed the skepticism about metaphysical doctrines that would characterize his entire religious career. How could the state of 'Nothingness' be the unconditioned and uncreated Self, when he knew perfectly well that he had manufactured this experience for himself? This 'Nothingness' could not be absolute, because he had brought it about by means of his own yogic expertise. Gotama was ruthlessly honest and would not allow himself to be gulled by an interpretation that was not warranted by the facts. The elevated state of consciousness that he had achieved could not be Nibbāṇa, because when he came out of his trance, he was still subject to passion, desire and craving. He had remained his unregenerate, greedy self. He had not been permanently transformed by the experience and had attained no lasting peace. Nibbāṇa could not be temporary! That would be a contradiction in terms, since Nibbāṇa was eternal.[32] The transitory nature of our ordinary lives was one of the chief signs of *dukkha* and a constant source of pain.

But Gotama was ready to give this reading of the yogic experience one last try. The plane of 'nothingness' was not the highest *āyatana.* There was a fourth plane, called 'neither-perception-nor-nonperception.' It could be that this highly refined state did lead to the Self. He heard that another yogin called Uddaka Rāmaputta had achieved the rare distinction of reaching this exalted *āyatana,* so he went to join his *sangha* in the hope that Uddaka could guide him to this peak yogic trance. Yet again, he was successful, but when he came back to himself, Gotama still found that he was prey to desire, fear and suffering. He could not accept Uddaka's explanation that when he had entered this final yogic plane he had experienced the Self.[33] Was what these mystics called the eternal Self perhaps simply another delusion? All that this type of yoga could do was give practitioners a brief respite from suffering. The metaphysical doctrine of Sāṃkhya-Yoga had failed him, since it could not bring even a gifted yogin any final release.

So Gotama abandoned yoga for a time and turned to asceticism (*tapas*), which some of the forest-monks believed could burn up all negative *kamma* and lead to liberation. He joined forces with five other ascetics and they practiced their exacting penances together, though sometimes Gotama sought seclusion, running frantically through the groves and thickets if he so much as glimpsed a shepherd on the horizon. During this period, Gotama went either naked or clad in the roughest hemp. He slept out in the open during the freezing winter nights, lay on a mattress of spikes and even fed on his own urine and feces. He held his breath for so long that his head seemed to split and there was a fearful roaring in his ears. He stopped eating and his bones stuck out 'like a row of spindles . . . or the beams of an old shed.' When he touched his stomach, he could almost feel his spine. His hair fell out and his skin became black and withered. At one point, some passing gods saw him lying by the roadside, showing so few signs of life that they thought he had died. But all this was in vain. However severe his austerities, perhaps even because of them, his body still clamored for attention, and he was still plagued by lust and craving. In fact, he seemed more conscious of himself than ever.[34]

Finally, Gotama had to face the fact that asceticism had proved as fruitless as yoga. All he had achieved after this heroic assault upon his egotism was a prominent rib cage and a dangerously weakened body. He might easily have died and still not attained the peace of Nibbāṇa. He and his five companions were living near Uruvelā at this time, on the banks of the broad Nerañjarā river. He was aware that the other five *bhikkhus* looked up to him as their leader, and were certain that he would be the first to achieve the final release from sorrow and rebirth. Yet he had failed them. Nobody, he told himself, could have subjected himself to more grueling penances, but instead of extricating himself from his human limitations, he had simply manufactured more suffering for himself. He had come to the end of the road. He had tried, to the best of his considerable abilities, the accepted ways to achieve enlightenment, but none of them had worked. The *dhammas* taught by the great teachers of the day seemed fundamentally flawed; many of their practitioners looked as sick, miserable and haggard as himself.[35] Some people would have despaired, given up the quest, and returned to the comfortable life they had left behind. A householder might be doomed to rebirth, but so, it seemed, were the ascetics who had 'Gone Forth' from society.

The yogins, ascetics and forest-monks had all realized that the self-conscious and eternally greedy ego was at the root of the problem. Men and women seemed chronically preoccupied with themselves, and this made it impossible for them to enter the realm of sacred peace. In various ways, they had tried to vanquish this egotism and get below the restless flux of conscious states and unconscious *vāsanās* to an absolute principle, which, they believed, they would find in the depths of the psyche. Yogins and ascetics in particular had tried to retreat from the profane world, so that they became impervious to external conditions and sometimes seemed scarcely alive. They understood how dangerous egotism could be and tried to mitigate it with the ideal of *ahiṃsā,* but it seemed to be almost impossible to extinguish this selfishness. None of these methods had worked for Gotama; they had left his secular self unchanged; he was still plagued by desire and still immersed in the toils of consciousness. He had begun to wonder if the sacred Self was a delusion. He was, perhaps, beginning to think that it was not a helpful symbol of the eternal, unconditioned Reality he sought. To seek an enhanced Self might even endorse the egotism that he needed to abolish. Nevertheless Gotama had not lost hope. He was still certain that it was possible for human beings to reach the final liberation of enlightenment. Henceforth, he would rely solely on his own insights. The established forms of spirituality had failed him, so he decided to strike out on his own and to accept the *dhamma* of no other teacher. 'Surely,' he cried, 'there must be another way to achieve enlightenment!'[36]

And at that very moment, when he seemed to have come to a dead end, the beginning of a new solution declared itself to him.

3 ENLIGHTENMENT

THE LEGENDS INDICATE that Gotama's childhood had been spent in an unawakened state, locked away from that knowledge of suffering which alone can bring us to spiritual maturity, but in later years he recalled that there had been one moment which had given him intimations of another mode of being. His father had taken him to watch the ceremonial ploughing of the fields before the planting of the next year's crop. All the men of the villages and townships took part in this annual event, so Suddhodana had left his small son in the care of his nurses under the shade of a rose-apple tree while he went to work. But the nurses decided to go and watch the ploughing, and, finding himself alone, Gotama sat up. In one version of this story, we are told that when he looked at the field that was being ploughed, he noticed that the young grass had been torn up and that insects and the eggs they had laid in these new shoots had been destroyed. The little boy gazed at the carnage and felt a strange sorrow, as though it were his own relatives that had been killed.[1] But it was a beautiful day, and a feeling of pure joy rose up unbidden in his heart. We have all experienced such moments, which come upon us unexpectedly and without any striving on our part. Indeed, as soon as we start to reflect upon our happiness, ask why we are so joyful and become self-conscious, the experience fades. When we bring self into it, this unpremeditated joy cannot last: it is essentially a moment of ecstasy, a rapture which takes us outside the body and beyond the prison of our own egotism. Such *exstasis,* a word that literally means 'to stand outside the self,' has nothing to do with the craving and greed that characterize so much of our waking lives. As Gotama reflected later, it 'existed apart from objects that awaken *tanhā.*' The child had been taken out of himself by a moment of spontaneous compassion, when he had allowed the pain of creatures that had nothing to do with him personally to pierce him to the heart. This surge of selfless empathy had brought him a moment of spiritual release.

Instinctively, the boy composed himself and sat in the *āsana* position, with straight back and crossed legs. A natural yogin, he entered into the first *jhāna,* a trance in which the meditator feels a calm happiness but is still able to think and reflect.[2] Nobody had taught him the techniques of yoga, but for a few moments, the child had a taste of what it might be like to leave himself behind. The commentary tells us that the natural world recognized the spiritual potential of the young Gotama. As the day wore on, the shadows of the other trees moved, but not the shade of the rose-apple tree, which continued to shield the boy from the blazing sun. When the nurses came back, they were stunned by the miracle and fetched Suddhodana, who paid homage to the little boy. These last elements are certainly fictional, but the story of the trance, historical or not, is important in the Pāli legend and is said to have played a crucial role in Gotama's enlightenment.

Years later, just after he had cried, with mingled optimism and despair, 'Surely there must be another way to enlightenment!', Gotama recalled this childhood experience. At that moment – again, unpremeditated and unsought – the memory of that childhood ecstasy rose to the surface of his mind. Emaciated, exhausted and dangerously ill, Gotama remembered the 'cool shade of the rose-apple tree,' which, inevitably, brought to mind the 'coolness' of Nibbāṇa. Most yogins could only achieve the first *jhāna* after years of study and hard work, but it had come to him without any effort on his part and given him a foretaste of Nibbāṇa. Ever since he had left Kapilavatthu, he had shunned all happiness as part of his campaign against desire. During his years as an ascetic, he had almost destroyed his body, hoping that he could thereby force himself into the sacred world that was the inverse of humanity's usual suffering existence. Yet as a child he had attained that yogic ecstasy without any trouble at all, after an experience of pure joy. As he reflected on the coolness of the rose-apple tree, he imagined, in his weakened state, the relief of being convalescent (*nibbuta*), after a lifetime of fever. Then he was struck by an extraordinary idea. 'Could this,' he asked himself, 'possibly be the way to enlightenment?' Had the other teachers been wrong? Instead of torturing our reluctant selves into the final release, we might be able to achieve it effortlessly and spontaneously. Could Nibbāṇa be built into the structure of our humanity? If an untrained child could reach the first *jhāna* and have intimations of Nibbāṇa without even trying, then yogic insight must be profoundly natural to human beings. Instead of making yoga an assault upon humanity, perhaps it could be used to cultivate innate tendencies that led to *ceto-vimutti*, the 'release of the mind' that was a synonym for the supreme enlightenment?

As soon as he had mulled over the details of that childhood experience, Gotama became convinced that his hunch was correct. This was indeed the way to Nibbāṇa. Now all he had to do was prove it. What had produced that mood of calm happiness that had modulated so easily into the first *jhāna*? An essential element had been what Gotama called 'seclusion.' He had been left alone; he could never have entered the ecstatic state if his nurses had distracted him with their chatter. Meditation required privacy and silence. But this seclusion went beyond physical solitude. Sitting under the rose-apple tree, his mind had been separated from desire for material things and from anything unwholesome and unprofitable. Since he had left home six years before, Gotama had been fighting his human nature and crushing its every impulse. He had come to distrust any kind of pleasure. But, he now asked himself, why should he be afraid of the type of joy he had experienced on that long-ago afternoon? That pure delight had had nothing to do with greedy craving or sensual desire. Some joyful experiences could actually lead to an abandonment of egotism and to the achievement of an exalted yogic state. Again, as soon as he had posed the question to himself, Gotama responded with his usual, confident decisiveness: 'I am not afraid of such pleasures,' he said.[3] The secret was to reproduce the seclusion that had led to his trance, and foster such wholesome (*kusala*) states of mind as the disinterested compassion that had made him grieve for the insects and the shoots of young grass. At the same time, he would carefully avoid any state of mind that would not be helpful or would impede his enlightenment.

He had, of course, already been behaving along these lines by observing the 'five prohibitions' which had forbidden such 'unhelpful' (*akusala*) activities as violence, lying, stealing, intoxication and sex. But now, he realized, this was not enough. He must cultivate the positive attitudes that were the opposite of these five restraints. Later, he would say that a person seeking enlightenment must be 'energetic, resolute and persevering' in pursuing those 'helpful,' 'wholesome' or 'skillful' (*kusala*) states that would promote spiritual health. *Ahiṃsā* (harmlessness) could only take one part of the way: instead of simply avoiding violence, an aspirant must behave gently and kindly to everything and everybody; he must cultivate thoughts of loving-kindness to counter any incipient feelings of ill will. It was very important not to tell lies, but it was also crucial to engage in 'right talk' and make sure that whatever you said was worth saying: 'reasoned, accurate, clear, and beneficial.' Besides refraining from stealing, a *bhikkhu* should positively rejoice in taking whatever alms he was given, expressing no personal preference, and should take delight in possessing the bare minimum.[4] The yogins had always maintained that avoiding the five prohibitions would lead to 'infinite happiness,' but by deliberately cultivating these positive states of mind, such *exstasis* could surely be redoubled. Once this 'skillful' behavior became so habitual that it was second nature, the aspirant, Gotama believed, would 'feel within himself a pure joy,' similar to if not identical with the bliss that he had felt as a boy under the rose-apple tree.[5]

This almost Proustian recollection was, according to the texts, a turning point for Gotama. He resolved from then on to work with human nature and not fight against it – amplifying states of mind that were conducive to enlightenment and turning his back on anything that would stunt his potential. Gotama was developing what he called a 'Middle Way,' which shunned physical and emotional self-indulgence on the one hand, and extreme asceticism (which could be just as destructive) on the other. He decided that he must immediately abandon the punitive regime that he had followed with his five companions, which had made him so ill that there was no way he could experience the 'pure joy' that was a prelude to liberation. For the first time in months, he took solid food, starting with what the texts call *kummāsa*, a soothing milky junket or rice pudding. When the five *bhikkhus* saw him eating, they were horrified and walked away in disgust, convinced that Gotama had abandoned the struggle for enlightenment.[6]

But this, of course, was not the case. Gotama must have nursed himself slowly back to health, and during this time he probably started to develop his own special kind of yoga. He was no longer hoping to discover his eternal Self, since he was beginning to think that this Self was just another one of the delusions that held people back from enlightenment. His yoga was designed to help him become better acquainted with his human nature, so that he could make it work for him in the attainment of Nibbāṇa. First, as a preliminary to meditation, came the practice that he called 'mindfulness' (*sati*), in which he scrutinized his behavior at every moment of the day. He noted the ebb and flow of his feelings and sensations, together with the fluctuations of his consciousness. If sensual desire arose, instead of simply crushing it, he took note of what had given rise to it and how soon it faded away. He observed the way his senses and thoughts interacted with the external world, and made himself conscious of his every bodily action. He would become aware of the way he walked, bent down or stretched his limbs, and of his behavior while 'eating, drinking, chewing, and tasting, in defecating, walking, standing, sitting, sleeping, waking, speaking and keeping silent.'[7] He noticed the way ideas coursed through his mind and the constant stream of desires and irritations that could plague him in a brief half-hour. He became 'mindful' of the way he responded to a sudden noise or a change in the temperature, and saw how quickly even a tiny thing disturbed his peace of mind. This 'mindfulness' was not cultivated in a spirit of neurotic introspection. Gotama had not put his humanity under the microscope in this way in order to castigate himself for his 'sins.' Sin had no place in his system, since any guilt would simply be 'unhelpful': it would embed an aspirant in the ego that he was trying to transcend. Gotama's use of the words *kusala* and *akusala* are significant. Sex, for example, was not listed among the five *yama* because it was sinful, but because it would not help a person reach Nibbāṇa; sex was emblematic of the desire that imprisoned human beings in *saṃsāra*; it expended energy that would be better employed in yoga. A *bhikkhu* refrained from sex as an athlete might abstain from certain foods before an important competition. Sex had its uses, but it was not 'helpful' to one engaged in the 'noble quest.' Gotama was not observing his human nature in order to pounce on his failings, but was becoming acquainted with the way it worked in order to exploit its capacities. He had become convinced that the solution to the problem of suffering lay within himself, in what he called 'this fathom-long carcass, this body and mind.'[8] Deliverance would come from the refinement of his own mundane nature, and so he must investigate it and get to know it as intimately as an equestrian learns to know the horse he is training.

But the practice of mindfulness also made him more acutely aware than ever of the pervasiveness of both suffering and the desire that gave rise to it. All these thoughts and longings that crowded into his consciousness were of such short duration. Everything was impermanent (*anicca*). However intense a craving might be, it soon petered out and was replaced by something quite different. Nothing lasted long, not even the bliss of meditation. The transitory nature of life was one of the chief causes of suffering, and as he recorded his feelings, moment by moment, Gotama also became aware that the *dukkha* of life was not confined to the major traumas of sickness, old age and death. It happened on a daily, even hourly basis, in all the little disappointments, rejections, frustrations and failures that befall us in the course of a single day: 'Pain, grief and despair are *dukkha,*' he would explain later, 'being forced into proximity with what we hate is suffering, being separated from what we love is suffering, not getting what we want is suffering.'[9] True, there was pleasure in life, but once Gotama had subjected this to the merciless scrutiny of mindfulness, he noticed how often our satisfaction meant suffering for others. The prosperity of one person usually depends upon the poverty or exclusion of somebody else; when we get something that makes us happy, we immediately start to worry about losing it; we pursue an object of desire, even when we know in our heart of hearts that it will make us unhappy in the long run.

Mindfulness also made Gotama highly sensitive to the prevalence of the desire or craving that is the cause of this suffering. The ego is voracious and continually wants to gobble up other things and people. We almost never see things as they are in themselves, but our vision is colored by whether we want them or not, how we can get them, or how they can bring us profit. Our view of the world is, therefore, distorted by our greed, and this often leads to ill will and enmity, when our desires clash with the cravings of others. Henceforth, Gotama would usually couple 'desire' (*tanhā*) with 'hatred' (*dosa*). When we say 'I want,' we often find ourselves filled with envy, jealousy and rage if other people block our desires or succeed where we have failed. Such states of mind are 'unskillful' because they make us more selfish than ever. Desire and hatred, its concomitant, are thus the joint cause of much of the misery and evil in the world. On the one hand, desire makes us 'grab' or 'cling' to things that can never give lasting satisfaction. On the other, it makes us constantly discontented with our present circumstances. As Gotama observed the way one craving after another took possession of his mind and heart, he noticed how human beings were ceaselessly yearning to become something else, go somewhere else, and acquire something they do not have. It is as though they were continually seeking a form of rebirth, a new kind of existence. Craving (*tanhā*) manifests itself even in the desire to change our physical position, go into another room, have a snack or suddenly leave work and go find somebody to talk to. These petty cravings assail us hour by hour, minute by minute, so that we know no rest. We are consumed and distracted by the compulsion to become something different. 'The world, whose very nature is to change, is constantly determined to become something else,' Gotama concluded. 'It is at the mercy of change, it is only happy when it is caught up in the process of change, but this love of change contains a measure of fear, and this fear itself is *dukkha*.'[10]

But when Gotama reflected upon these truths, he was not doing so in an ordinary, discursive manner. He brought the techniques of yoga to bear upon them, so that they became more vivid and immediate than any conclusion arrived at by normal ratiocination. Every day, after he had collected enough alms for his daily meal, which he usually took before noon, Gotama would seek out a secluded spot, sit down in the *āsana* posture and begin the yogic exercises of *ekāgratā* or concentration.[11] He would practice this mindfulness in a yogic context and, as a result, his insights gained a new clarity. He could see them 'directly,' enter into them and learn to observe them without the filter of self-protecting egotism that distorts them. Human beings do not usually want to realize the pervasiveness of pain, but now Gotama was learning, with the skill of a trained yogin, to 'see things as they really are.' He did not, however, stop at these more negative truths; he was also fostering the 'skillful' states with the same intensity. A person, he explained later, could purify his or her mind by cultivating these positive and helpful states while performing the yogic exercises, sitting cross-legged and, by means of the respiratory discipline of *prāṇāyāma,* inducing an alternative state of consciousness.

> Once he has banished malevolence and hatred from his mind, he lives without ill will and is also full of compassion, desiring the welfare of all living beings.... Once he has banished the mental habits of laziness and indolence, he is not only free of laziness and indolence but has a mind that is lucid, conscious of itself and completely alert;... Once he has banished anxiety and worry, he lives without anxiety and his mind becomes calm and still;... Once he has banished uncertainty, he lives with a mind that has outgrown debilitating doubt and is no longer plagued by unprofitable [*akusala*] mental states.

In this way, a yogin 'purifies his mind' of hatred, indolence, anxiety and uncertainty.[12] The *brahmins* had believed that they achieved this kind of spiritual purification by means of the ritual *kamma* of animal sacrifice. But now Gotama realized that anybody could cultivate this purity, without the agency of a priest, by means of the mental *kamma* of meditation, which could, he believed, if performed at sufficient depth in the yogic manner, transform the restless and destructive tendencies of the conscious and unconscious mind.

In later years, Gotama claimed that the new yogic method he had developed brought to birth a wholly different kind of human being, one who was not dominated by craving, greed and egotism. It was, he explained, like a sword being drawn from its scabbard or a snake from its slough: 'the sword and the snake were one thing; the slough and scabbard had been something quite different.'[13] In his system, meditation would take the place of sacrifice; at the same time, the discipline of compassion would take the place of the old punitive asceticism (*tapas*). Compassion, he was convinced, would also give the aspirant access to hitherto-unknown dimensions of his humanity. When Gotama had studied yoga with Ālāra Kālāma, he had learned to ascend to a higher state of consciousness through the four successive *jhāna* states: each trance had brought the yogin greater spiritual insight and refinement. Now Gotama transformed these four *jhānas* by fusing them with what he called 'the immeasurables' (*appamana*). Every day in meditation he would deliberately evoke the emotion of love – 'that huge, expansive and immeasurable feeling that knows no hatred' – and direct it to each of the four corners of the world. He did not omit a single living thing – plant, animal, demon, friend or foe – from this radius of benevolence. In the first 'immeasurable,' which corresponded to the first *jhāna,* he cultivated a feeling of friendship for everybody and everything. When he had mastered this, he progressed to the cultivation of compassion with the second *jhāna,* learning to suffer with other people and things and to empathize with their pain, as he had felt the suffering of the grass and the insects under the rose-apple tree. When he reached the third *jhāna,* he fostered a 'sympathetic joy' which rejoices at the happiness of others, without reflecting upon how this might redound upon himself. Finally, when he attained the fourth *jhāna,* in which the yogin was so immersed in the object of his contemplation that he was beyond pain or pleasure, Gotama aspired to an attitude of total equanimity toward others, feeling neither attraction nor antipathy.[14] This was a very difficult state, since it required the yogin to divest himself completely of that egotism which always looks to see how other things and people can be of benefit or detriment to oneself; it demanded that he abandon all personal preference and adopt a wholly disinterested benevolence. Where traditional yoga had built up in the yogin a state of impervious autonomy, so that the yogin became increasingly heedless of the world, Gotama was learning to transcend himself in an act of total compassion toward all other beings, infusing the old disciplines with loving-kindness.

The purpose of both mindfulness and the immeasurables was to neutralize the power of that egotism that limits human potential. Instead of saying 'I want,' the yogin would learn to seek the good of others; instead of succumbing to the hatred that is the result of our self-centered greed, Gotama was mounting a compassionate offensive of benevolence and goodwill. When these positive, skillful states were cultivated with yogic intensity, they could root themselves more easily in the unconscious impulses of our minds and become habitual. The immeasurables were designed to pull down the barricades we erect between ourselves and others in order to protect the fragile ego; they sought a larger reach of being and enhanced horizons. As the mind broke free of its normal, selfish constriction and embraced all beings, it was felt to have become 'expansive, without limits, enhanced, without hatred or petty malevolence.' The consciousness now felt as infinite as the sound made by an expert conch-blower, which was thought to pervade all space. If taken to a very high level, this yoga of compassion (*karuṇā*) yielded a 'release of the mind' (*ceto-vimutti*), a phrase which, in the Pāli texts, is used of enlightenment itself.[15] Through the discipline of mindfulness too, Gotama began to experience a deepening calm, especially when this was accompanied by *prāṇāyāma.* He was beginning to discover what it was like to live without the selfish cravings that poison our lives and our relations with others, imprisoning us within the petty confines of our own needs and desires. He was also becoming less affected by these unruly yearnings. It has been found that this habit of attentive self-scrutiny has helped Buddhist practitioners to monitor the distractions that deprive us of peace; as the meditator becomes aware of the ephemeral nature of those invasive thoughts and cravings, it becomes difficult to identify with them or to see them in any way as 'mine.' Consequently they become less disturbing.[16]

We do not know how long it took Gotama to recover his health after his years of asceticism. The scriptures speed up the process to make it more dramatic, and give the impression that Gotama was ready for the final struggle with himself after one bowl of junket. This cannot have been true. The effects of mindfulness and the cultivation of skillful states take time. Gotama himself said that it could take at least seven years, and stressed that the new self developed imperceptibly over a long period. 'Just as the ocean slopes gradually, falls away gradually, and shelves gradually with no sudden incline,' he later warned his disciples, 'so in this method, training, discipline and practice take effect by slow degrees, with no sudden perception of the ultimate truth.'[17] The texts show Gotama attaining his supreme enlightenment and becoming a Buddha in a single night, because they are less concerned with historical fact than with tracing the general contours of the process of achieving release and inner peace.

Thus in one of the oldest portions of the scriptures, we read that after Gotama had been deserted by his five companions and had been nourished by his first meal, he set off toward Uruvelā, walking there by easy stages. When he reached Senānigāma beside the Nerañjarā river, he noticed 'an agreeable plot of land, a pleasant grove, a sparkling river with delightful and smooth banks, and, nearby, a village whose inhabitants would feed him.'[18] This, Gotama thought, was just the place to undertake the final effort that would bring him enlightenment. If he was to reproduce the calm content that had modulated so easily into the first *jhāna* under the rose-apple tree, it was important to find a congenial spot for his meditation. He sat down, tradition has it, under a bodhi tree, and took up the *āsana* position, vowing that he would not leave this spot until he had attained Nibbāṇa. This pleasant grove is now known as Bodh Gaya and is an important site of pilgrimage, because it is thought to be the place where Gotama experienced the *yathabhuta,* his enlightenment or awakening. It was in this spot that he became a Buddha.

It was late spring. Scholars have traditionally dated the enlightenment of Gotama at about the year 528 B.C.E., though recently some have argued for a later date in the first half of the fifth century. The Pāli texts give us some information about what happened that night, but nothing that makes much sense to an outsider who has not been through the Buddhist regimen. They say that Gotama mused upon the deeply conditional nature of all life as we know it, saw all his past lives, and recovered that 'secluded' and solitary state he had experienced as a child. He then slipped easily into the first *jhāna*, and progressed through ever higher states of consciousness until he gained an insight that forever transformed him and convinced him that he had freed himself from the round of *saṃsāra* and rebirth.[19] But there seems little new about this insight, traditionally known as the Four Noble Truths and regarded as the fundamental teaching of Buddhism. The first of these verities was the noble truth of suffering *(dukkha)* that informs the whole of human life. The second truth was that the cause of this suffering was desire (*tanhā*). In the third noble truth, Gotama asserted that Nibbāṇa existed as a way out of this predicament and finally, he claimed that he had discovered the path that leads from suffering and pain to its cessation in the state of Nibbāṇa.

There seems nothing strikingly original about these truths. Most of the monks and ascetics of North India would have agreed with the first three, and Gotama himself had been convinced of them since the very beginning of his quest. If there is anything novel, it was the fourth truth, in which Gotama proclaimed that he had found a way to enlightenment, a method which he called the Noble Eightfold Path. Its eight components have been rationalized still further into a threefold plan of action, consisting of morality, meditation and wisdom:

[1] *Morality* (*sila*), which consists of right speech, right action and right livelihood. This essentially comprises the cultivation of the 'skillful' states in the way we have discussed.

[2] *Meditation* (*samādhi*), which comprises Gotama's revised yoga disciplines, under the headings of right effort, mindfulness and concentration.

[3] *Wisdom* (*paññā*): the two virtues of right understanding and

right resolve enable an aspirant, by means of morality and meditation, to understand the Buddha's Dhamma, enter into it 'directly' and integrate it into his or her daily life in the way that we shall discuss in the following chapter.

If there is any truth to the story that Gotama gained enlightenment at Bodh Gayā in a single night, it could be that he acquired a sudden, absolute certainty that he really *had* discovered a method that would, if followed energetically, bring an earnest seeker to Nibbāṇa. He had not made this up; it was not a new creation or an invention of his own. On the contrary, he always insisted that he had simply discovered 'a path of great antiquity, an ancient trail, traveled by human beings in a far-off, distant era.'[20] The other Buddhas, his predecessors, had taught this path an immeasurably long time ago, but this ancient knowledge had faded over the years and had been entirely forgotten. Gotama insisted that this insight was simply a statement of things 'as they really are'; the path was written into the very structure of existence. It was, therefore, *the* Dhamma, par excellence, because it elucidated the fundamental principles that govern the life of the cosmos. If men, women, animals and gods kept to this path, they could all attain an enlightenment that would bring them peace and fulfillment, because they were no longer struggling against their deepest grain.

But it must also be understood that the Four Noble Truths do not present a theory that can be judged by the rational intellect alone; they are not simply notional verities. The Buddha's Dhamma was essentially a method, and it stands or falls not by its metaphysical acuity or its scientific accuracy, but by the extent to which it works. The truths claim to bring suffering to an end, not because people subscribe to a salvific creed and to certain beliefs, but because they adopt Gotama's program or way of life. Over the centuries, men and women have indeed found that this regimen has brought them a measure of peace and insight. The Buddha's claim, echoed by all the other great sages of the Axial Age, was that by reaching beyond themselves to a reality that transcends their rational understanding, men and women become fully human. The Buddha never claimed that his knowledge of the Four Noble Truths was unique, but that he was the first person, in this present era, to have 'realized' them and made them a reality in his own life. He found that he *had* extinguished the craving, hatred and ignorance that hold humanity in thrall. He *had* attained Nibbāṇa, and even though he was still subject to physical ailments and other vicissitudes, nothing could touch his inner peace or cause him serious mental pain. His method had worked. 'The holy life has been lived out to its conclusion!' he cried out triumphantly at the end of that momentous night under the bodhi tree. 'What had to be done has been accomplished; there is nothing else to do!'[21]

Those of us who do not live according to the Buddhist program of morality and meditation have, therefore, no means of judging this claim. The Buddha was always quite clear that his Dhamma could not be understood by rational thinking alone. It only revealed its true significance when it was apprehended 'directly,' according to yogic methods, and in the right ethical context.[22] The Four Noble Truths do make logical sense, but they do not become compelling until an aspirant has learned to identify with them at a profound level and has integrated them with his own life. Then and only then will he experience the 'exultation,' 'joy' and 'serenity' which, according to the Pāli texts, come to us when we divest ourselves of egotism, liberate ourselves from the prison of self-centeredness, and see the Truths 'as they really are.'[23] Without the meditation and morality prescribed by the Buddha, the Truths remain as abstract as a musical score, which for most of us cannot reveal its true beauty on the page but needs to be orchestrated and interpreted by a skilled performer.

Even though the Truths make rational sense, the texts emphasize that they did not come to Gotama by means of discursive reasoning. As he sat meditating under the bodhi tree, they 'rose up' in him, as from the depths of his being. He apprehended them within himself by the kind of 'direct knowledge' acquired by a yogin who practices the disciplines of yoga with 'diligence, ardor and self-control.' Gotama was so absorbed in these Truths, the object of his contemplation, that nothing interposed itself between them and his own mind and heart. He had become their human embodiment. When people observed the way he behaved and responded to events, they could see what the Dhamma was like; they could see Nibbāṇa in human form. In order to share Gotama's experience, we have to approach the Truths in a spirit of total self-abandonment. We have to be prepared to leave our old unregenerate selves behind. The compassionate morality and yoga devised by Gotama only brought liberation if the aspirant was ready to lay aside all egotism. It is significant that at the moment he achieved Nibbāṇa under the bodhi tree, Gotama did not cry 'I am liberated,' but 'It is liberated!'[24] He had transcended himself, achieved an *exstasis,* and discovered an enhanced 'immeasurable' dimension of his humanity that he had not known before.

What did the new Buddha mean when he claimed to have reached Nibbāṇa on that spring night? Had he himself, as the word implied, been 'snuffed out,' extinguished like a candle flame? During his six-year quest, Gotama had not masochistically courted annihilation but had sought enlightenment. He had wanted to wake up to his full potential as a human person, not to be wiped out. Nibbāṇa did not mean personal extinction: what had been snuffed out was not his personality but the fires of greed, hatred and delusion. As a result, he enjoyed a blessed 'coolness' and peace. By tamping out the 'unhelpful' states of mind, the Buddha had gained the peace which comes from selflessness; it is a condition that those of us who are still enmeshed in the cravings of egotism, which make us hostile toward others and distort our vision, cannot imagine. That is why the Buddha always refused, in the years following his enlightenment, to define or describe Nibbāṇa: it would, he said, be 'improper' to do so, because there are no words to describe such a state to an unenlightened person.[25] The attainment of Nibbāṇa did not mean that the Buddha would never experience any more suffering. He would grow old, get sick and die like everybody else and would experience pain while doing so. Nibbāṇa does not give an awakened person trancelike immunity, but an inner haven which enables a man or woman to live *with* pain, to take possession of it, affirm it, and experience a profound peace of mind in the midst of suffering. Nibbāṇa, therefore, is found within oneself, in the very heart of each person's being. It is an entirely natural state; it is not bestowed by grace nor achieved for us by a supernatural savior; it can be reached by anybody who cultivates the path to enlightenment as assiduously as Gotama did. Nibbāṇa is a still center; it gives meaning to life. People who lose touch with this quiet place and do not orient their lives toward it can fall apart. Artists, poets and musicians can only become fully creative if they work from this inner core of peace and integrity. Once a person has learned to access this nucleus of calm, he or she is no longer driven by conflicting fears and desires, and is able to face pain, sorrow and grief with equanimity. An enlightened or awakened human being has discovered a strength within that comes from being correctly centered, beyond the reach of selfishness.

Once he had found this inner realm of calm, which is Nibbāṇa, Gotama had become a Buddha. He was convinced that, once egotism had been snuffed out, there would be no flames or fuel to spark a new existence, because the desire (*tanhā*) which bound him to *saṃsāra* had been finally quenched. When he died, he would attain his *paranibbāṇa*, his final rest. Again, this did not mean total extinction, as Westerners sometimes assume. The *paranibbāṇa* was a mode of existence that we cannot conceive unless we have become enlightened ourselves. There are no words or concepts for it, because our language is derived from the sense data of our unhappy, mundane existence; we cannot really imagine a life in which there is no egotism of any kind. But that does not mean that such an existence is impossible; it became a Buddhist heresy to maintain that an enlightened person would cease to exist after death.[26] In the same way, monotheists have insisted that there are no words that can adequately describe the reality they call 'God.' 'He who has gone to his final rest (*parinibbāṇa*) cannot be defined by any measure,' the Buddha would tell his followers in later life. 'There are no words capable of describing him. What thought might comprehend has been canceled out, and so has every mode of speech.'[27] In purely mundane terms, Nibbāṇa was 'nothing,' not because it did not exist, but because it corresponded to no thing that we know. But those who had, by dint of the disciplines of yoga and compassionate morality, managed to access this still center within found that they enjoyed an immeasurably richer mode of being, because they had learned to live without the limitations of egotism.

The account of the Buddha's attainment of enlightenment under the bodhi tree in the Pāli texts can leave the modern reader feeling baffled and frustrated. It is one of the places where these Theravādin scriptures become opaque to people who are not expert yogins, since they dwell in such detail on meditative technicalities. More helpful to an outsider is the story told in the later scripture, the *Nidāna Kathā*, which makes the notion of enlightenment more accessible to ordinary mortals. As with its version of Gotama's 'Going Forth,' this story explores the psychological and spiritual implications of enlightenment in a way that a lay person or Buddhist beginner can understand, because it has no yogic jargon but gives us a wholly mythological account of the enlightenment. The author is not attempting to write history in our sense, but draws instead on timeless imagery to show what is involved in the discovery of Nibbāṇa. He uses motifs common in mythology, which has been aptly described as a pre-modern form of psychology, tracing the inner paths of the psyche and making clearer the obscure world of the unconscious mind. Buddhism is an essentially psychological religion, so it is not surprising that the early Buddhist authors made such skillful use of mythology.[28] Again, we must recall that none of these texts is concerned with telling us what actually happened, but rather is intended to help the audience gain their own enlightenment.

The *Nidāna Kathā* emphasizes the need for courage and determination: it shows Gotama engaged in a heroic struggle against all those forces within himself which militate against the achievement of Nibbāṇa. We read that after Gotama had eaten his dish of junket, he strode as majestically as a lion toward the bodhi tree to make his last bid for liberation, determined to reach his goal that very night. First, he circled the tree, trying to find the place where all the previous Buddhas had sat when they had won through to Nibbāṇa, but wherever he stood, 'the broad earth heaved and sunk, as though it was a huge cartwheel lying on its hub, and somebody was treading on its rim.'[29] Eventually, Gotama approached the eastern side of the tree, and when he stood there, the ground remained still. Gotama decided that this must be the 'immovable spot' on which all the previous Buddhas had positioned themselves, so he sat down in the *āsana* position facing the east, the region of the dawn, in the firm expectation that he was about to begin a new era in the history of humanity. 'Let my skin and sinews and bones dry up, together with all the flesh and blood of my body! I will welcome it!' Gotama vowed. 'But I will not move from this spot until I have attained the supreme and final wisdom.'[30]

The text emphasizes the fantastic shuddering of the earth as Gotama circled the bodhi tree to remind us not to read this story literally. This is not a physical location: the world-tree, standing at the axis of the cosmos, is a common feature of salvation mythology. It is the place where the divine energies pour into the world, where humanity encounters the Absolute and becomes more fully itself. We need only recall the cross of Jesus, which, according to Christian legend, stood on the same spot as the Tree of Knowledge of Good and Evil in the Garden of Eden. But in Buddhist myth, Gotama the man sits in this pivotal place, not a man-God, because human beings must save themselves without supernatural aid. The texts make it clear that Gotama had come to this axis of the universe, the mythological center that holds the whole of the cosmos together. The 'immovable spot' is that psychological state which enables us to see the world and ourselves in perfect balance. Without this psychological stability and this correct orientation, enlightenment is impossible: that is why all the Buddhas had to sit in this place – or achieve this state of mind – before they were able to attain Nibbāṇa. It is the Axis Mundi, the still point of calm where human beings, in many world myths, encounter the Real and the Unconditioned; it is the 'place' where things that seem diametrically opposed in the profane world come together in that *coincidentia oppositorum* that constitutes an experience of the Sacred. Life and death, emptiness and plenitude, physical and spiritual merge and conjoin, like the spokes of a wheel at its hub, in a way that is unimaginable to normal consciousness.[31] When Gotama had reached the state of perfect equilibrium that he had glimpsed as a child under the rose-apple tree, when his faculties were concentrated and his egotism under control, he was, he believed, ready to sit in the 'immovable spot.' He was at last in a position to receive the supreme insight.

But the struggle was not yet over. Gotama still had to fight those residual forces within himself which clung to the unregenerate life and did not want the ego to die. Māra, Gotama's shadow-self, appeared before him, decked out like a *cakkavatti,* a World Ruler, with a massive army. Māra himself was mounted on an elephant that was 150 leagues high. He had sprouted 1,000 arms, each of which brandished a deadly weapon. Māra's name means 'delusion.' He epitomized the ignorance which holds us back from enlightenment, since, as a *cakkavatti,* he could only envisage a victory achieved by physical force. Gotama was still not fully enlightened, so he tried to respond in kind, seeing the virtues he had acquired as defensive weapons, as a sword or a shield that would destroy this deadly army.[32] But, our author continues, despite Māra's power, Gotama was sitting in the 'unconquerable position,' proof against such vulgar coercion. When Māra hurled nine fearful storms against him, Gotama remained unmoved. The gods, who had gathered around to witness Gotama's attainment of Nibbāṇa, fled in terror, leaving him alone. When men and women seek salvation, in the Buddhist view, they can expect no divine support.

At this point, Māra approached Gotama and engaged him in a strange conversation. He told Gotama to 'arise from this seat; it does not belong to you, but to me.' Gotama, Māra thought, had transcended the world; he was invulnerable to all external opposition. But Māra was the Lord of this world, and it was he, the *cakkavatti,* who should sit at its pivotal center. He did not realize that the rage, hatred and violence that he had just exhibited disqualified him from taking up his position under the bodhi tree, which belongs only to the man who lives by compassion. Gotama pointed out that Māra was quite unprepared for enlightenment; he had never made any spiritual efforts, had never given alms, had never practiced yoga. So, Gotama concluded, 'this seat does not belong to you but to me.' He went on to add that in his previous lives he had given away all his possessions and had even laid down his life for others. What had Māra done? Could he produce witnesses to testify that he had performed such compassionate deeds? At once, Māra's soldiers cried as one man: 'I am his witness!' And Māra turned triumphantly to Gotama and asked him to validate his own claims.[33]

But Gotama was alone; he had no human being or god on his side who could act as a witness to his long preparation for enlightenment. He therefore did something that no *cakkavatti* would ever do: he asked for help. Reaching out with his right hand to touch the ground, he begged the earth to testify to his past acts of compassion. With a shattering roar, the earth replied: 'I bear you witness!' In terror, Māra's elephant fell to its knees and his soldiers deserted, running in fear in all directions.[34] The earth-witnessing posture, which shows the Buddha sitting in the cross-legged *āsana* position, touching the ground with his right hand, is a favorite icon in Buddhist art. It not only symbolizes Gotama's rejection of Māra's sterile machismo, but makes the profound point that a Buddha does indeed belong to the world. The Dhamma is exacting, but it is not against nature. There is a deep affinity between the earth and the selfless human being, something that Gotama had sensed when he recalled his trance under the rose-apple tree. The man or woman who seeks enlightenment is in tune with the fundamental structure of the universe. Even though the world seems to be ruled by the violence of Māra and his army, it is the compassionate Buddha who is most truly in tune with the basic laws of existence.

After this victory over Māra, which was really a victory over himself, there was nothing to hold Gotama back. The gods returned from the heavens and waited breathlessly for him to achieve his final release, for they needed his help as much as did any human being. Now Gotama entered the first *jhāna* and penetrated the inner world of his psyche; when he finally reached the peace of Nibbāṇa all the worlds of the Buddhist cosmos were convulsed, the heavens and hells shook, and the bodhi tree rained down red florets on the enlightened man. Throughout all the worlds,

> the flowering trees bloomed; the fruit trees were weighed down by the burden of their fruit; the trunk lotoses bloomed on the trunks of trees... The system of ten thousand worlds was like a bouquet of flowers sent whirling through the air.[35]

The ocean lost its salty taste, the blind and the deaf were able to see and hear; cripples could walk and the fetters of prisoners fell to the ground. Everything suddenly glimpsed new freedom and potency; for a few moments, each form of life was able to become more fully itself.

But the new Buddha could not save the world vicariously. Every single creature would have to put Gotama's program into practice to achieve its own enlightenment; he could not do it for them. Yet at first, it seemed that the Buddha, as we must now call Gotama, had decided against preaching the Dhamma that alone could save his fellow creatures. He would often be known as Sakyamūni, the Silent One from the republic of Sakka, because the knowledge he had acquired was ineffable and could not be described in words. Yet throughout the Ganges region, people were longing for a new spiritual vision, especially in the cities. This became clear, the Pāli texts tell us, almost immediately after the Buddha's enlightenment, when two passing merchants, called Tapussa and Bhalluka, who had been informed of the great event by one of the gods, came to the Buddha and paid homage to him. They became his first lay followers.[36] Yet despite this initial success, the Buddha was still reluctant. His Dhamma was too difficult to explain, he told himself; the people would not be prepared to undergo the arduous yogic and moral disciplines that it required. Far from wishing to renounce their craving, most people positively relished their attachments and would not want to hear his message of self-abandonment. 'If I taught the Dhamma,' the Buddha decided, 'people would not understand it and that would be exhausting and disappointing for me.'[37]

But then the god Brahma intervened; he had watched Gotama's enlightenment with close attention, and was devastated to hear this decision. If the Buddha refused to teach his

Dhamma, Brahma cried in dismay, 'the world will be lost, the world will not have a chance!' He decided to intervene. The Pāli texts introduce the gods into their narrative quite unselfconsciously. The gods were part of their universe, and these legends, which show Māra and Brahma contributing to the Buddha's story, illustrate the tolerant partnership that would exist between the new religion of Buddhism and the older cults. Unlike the Hebrew prophets, who poured scorn on the rival deities of their pagan neighbors, the early Buddhists felt no need to stamp out the traditional worship still enjoyed by vast numbers of people. Instead, the Buddha is shown allowing the gods to help him at certain key moments of his life. Like Māra, Brahma may also have represented an aspect of the Buddha's own personality. This was, perhaps, a way of suggesting that the gods were projections of subconscious human forces. The story of Brahma's intervention may indicate that there was a conflict within the Buddha's mind, and that while one part of him wanted to retire into solitude and enjoy the peace of Nibbāṇa undisturbed, there was another part of him that realized that he simply could not neglect his fellow creatures in this way.

In a complete reversal of their usual roles, Brahma left his heaven, descended to earth, and knelt before the new Buddha. 'Lord,' he prayed, 'please preach the Dhamma... there are people with only a little desire left within them who are pining for lack of this method; some of them will understand it.' He pleaded with the Buddha to 'look down at the human race which is drowning in pain and to travel far and wide to save the world.'[38] Compassion had been an essential component of the Buddha's enlightenment. One legend has it that Gotama was born from his mother's side at the level of her heart.[39] It is a parable – not, of course, to be taken literally

– of the birth of the spiritual human being. Only when we learn to live from the heart and to feel the suffering of others as if it were our own do we become truly human. Where a bestial man or woman puts self-interest first, a spiritual person learns to recognize and seeks to alleviate the pain of others. Many of us maintain ourselves in a state of deliberate heartlessness, a condition similar to the young Gotama's heavily defended pleasure-palace. But during his meditations and long preparation for Buddhahood, Gotama had opened his whole self to the fact of *dukkha* and allowed the reality of suffering to resonate within the deepest recesses of his being. He had made himself realize the Noble Truth of Suffering with 'direct knowledge,' until he had become one with it and integrated it wholly. He could not remain locked away safely in his private Nibbāṇa; he would thus be entering a new kind of pleasure-palace. Such a withdrawal would violate the essential dynamic of the Dhamma: the Buddha could not practice the four 'immeasurables,' sending out benevolent feelings to the four corners of the earth simply for his own spiritual benefit, while his fellow creatures languished in a world gone awry. One of the chief ways in which he had gained *ceto-vimutti*, the release of enlightenment, had been through the cultivation of loving-kindness and selfless empathy. The Dhamma demanded that he return to the marketplace and involve himself in the affairs of a sorrowing world.

To his great credit, the god Brahma (or the higher part of the Buddha's personality) realized this. The Buddha listened carefully to his plea and, the Pāli text tells us, 'out of compassion, he gazed upon the world with the eye of a Buddha.'[40] This is an important remark. A Buddha is not one who has simply attained his own salvation, but one who can sympathize with the suffering of others, even though he himself has won an immunity to pain. Now the Buddha realized that the gates of Nibbāṇa were 'wide open' to everybody; how could he close his heart to his fellows?[41] An essential part of the truth he had 'realized' under the bodhi tree was that to live morally was to live for others. He would spend the next forty-five years of his life tramping tirelessly through the cities and towns of the Ganges plain, bringing his Dhamma to gods, animals, men and women. There could be no limits to this compassionate offensive.

But who should be first to hear the message? The Buddha thought at once of his former teachers Ālāra Kālāma and Uddaka Rāmaputta, but some gods, who were waiting nearby, told him that they had both recently died. This was a great grief. His teachers had been good men who would certainly have understood his Dhamma; now, through no fault of their own, they had missed their chance and were condemned to yet another life of pain. This news could have given the Buddha a new sense of urgency. He next recalled the five *bhikkhus* who had practiced the penitential disciplines of *tapas* with him. They had fled from him in horror when he had taken his first meal, but he could not allow this rejection to cloud his judgment. He remembered how helpful and supportive they had been during their time together, and set out directly to find them. Hearing that they were now living in the Deer Park outside Vārānasī (the modern Benares), he began his journey, determined to set the Wheel of the Dhamma in motion and, as he put it, 'to beat the drum of the deathless Nibbāṇa.'[42] He did not expect much. The Buddha mistakenly believed that his teaching would only be followed for a few hundred years. But people had to be rescued, and the Buddha was compelled, by the very nature of the enlightenment that he had achieved, to do what he could for them.

4 DHAMMA

YET THE BUDDHA'S first attempt to teach was a complete failure. On his way to Gayā, he passed an acquaintance, Upaka, a Jain, who immediately noticed a change in his friend. 'How peaceful you look! How alert!' he exclaimed. 'You are so serene! Your complexion is clear, your eyes are bright! Who is your Teacher? and whose *dhamma* are you following these days?' It was a perfect opening. The Buddha explained that he had no teacher and belonged to no *sangha*. As yet, there was nobody like him in the world, because he had become an Arahant, an 'accomplished one' who had won through to the supreme enlightenment. 'What!' Upaka cried incredulously. 'Surely you are not saying that you are a Buddha, a Jina, a Spiritual Victor, the Holy One for whom we are all waiting?' Yes, the Buddha replied. He had conquered all craving and could indeed be called a Jina. Upaka looked at him skeptically and shook his head: 'Dream on, friend,' he said. 'I'm going this way.' Abruptly, he turned off the main road into a side track, refusing the direct route to Nibbāṇa.[1]

Undeterred, the Buddha continued his journey to Vārānasī, an important city and a center of learning for the *brahmins*. The Buddha did not linger in the town, however, but went straight to the Deer Park in the suburb of Isipatana, where he knew that his five former companions were living. When these *bhikkhus* saw him approaching they were alarmed. As far as they knew, Gotama, their old mentor, had abandoned the holy life and reverted to luxury and self-indulgence. They could no longer greet him as before, with the respect due to a great ascetic. But they were good men, dedicated to *ahiṃsā*, and did not want to hurt his feelings. Gotama, they decided, could sit with them for a while, if he wished, and rest after his long walk. But when the Buddha came closer, they were completely disarmed. Perhaps they too were struck by his new serenity and confidence, because one of the *bhikkhus* ran forward to greet him, taking his robe and his bowl, while the others prepared a seat, bringing water, a footstool and towel, so that their old leader could wash his feet. They greeted him with affection, calling him 'friend.'[2] This would often happen. The compassion and kindliness of the Buddha's manner would frequently defuse hostility in humans, gods and animals alike.

The Buddha came straight to the point. They should not really call him friend any more, he explained, because his old self had vanished and he had a wholly different status. He was now a Tathāgata, a curious title whose literal meaning is 'Thus Gone.' His egotism had been extinguished. They must not imagine that he had abandoned the holy life. Quite the reverse was true. There was a compelling conviction and urgency in his speech that his companions had never heard before. 'Listen!' he said, 'I have realized the undying state of Nibbāṇa. I will instruct you! I will teach you the Dhamma!'[3] If they listened to his teachings and put them into practice, they could become Arahants too; they could follow in his footsteps, entering into the supreme truth and making it a reality in their own lives. All they had to do was to give him a fair hearing.

The Buddha then preached his first sermon. It has been preserved in the texts as the *Dhammacakkappavattana-Sutta*, The Discourse that Set Rolling the Wheel of the Dhamma, because it brought the Teaching into the world and set in motion a new era for humanity, who now knew the correct way to live. Its purpose was not to impart abstruse metaphysical information, but to lead the five *bhikkhus* to enlightenment. They could become Arahants, like himself, but they would never equal their teacher, because the Buddha had achieved Nibbāṇa by himself, alone and unaided. He had then won further distinction, by making the decision to preach to the human race, becoming a Sammā Saṁbuddha, a Teacher of the Supreme Enlightenment. Later Buddhist teaching would maintain that a Sammā Saṁbuddha will only appear on earth every 32,000 years, when the knowledge of the Dhamma had completely faded from the earth. Gotama had become the Buddha of our age, and began his career in the Deer Park of Isipatana.

But what was he going to teach? The Buddha had no time for doctrines or creeds; he had no theology to impart, no theory about the root cause of *dukkha*, no tales of an Original Sin, and no definition of the Ultimate Reality. He saw no point in such speculations. Buddhism is disconcerting to those who equate faith with belief in certain inspired religious opinions. A person's theology was a matter of total indifference to the Buddha. To accept a doctrine on somebody else's authority was, in his eyes, an 'unskillful' state, which could not lead to enlightenment, because it was an abdication of personal responsibility. He saw no virtue in submitting to an official creed. 'Faith' meant trust that Nibbāṇa existed and a determination to prove it to oneself. The Buddha always insisted that his disciples test everything he taught them against their own experience and take nothing on hearsay. A religious idea could all too easily become a mental idol, one more thing to cling to, when the purpose of the *dhamma* was to help people to let go.

'Letting go' is one of the keynotes of the Buddha's teaching. The enlightened person did not grab or hold on to even the most authoritative instructions. Everything was transient and nothing lasted. Until his disciples recognized this in every fiber of their being, they would never reach Nibbāṇa. Even his own teachings must be jettisoned, once they had done their job. He once compared them to a raft, telling the story of a traveler who had come to a great expanse of water and desperately needed to get across. There was no bridge, no ferry, so he built a raft and rowed himself across the river. But then, the Buddha would ask his audience, what should the traveler do with the raft? Should he decide that because it had been so helpful to him, he should load it onto his back and lug it around with him wherever he went? Or should he simply moor it and continue his journey? The answer was obvious. 'In just the same way, *bhikkhus,* my teachings are like a raft, to be used to cross the river and not to be held on to,' the Buddha concluded. 'If you understand their raft-like nature correctly, you will even give up good teachings (*dhamma*), not to mention bad ones!'[4] His Dhamma was wholly pragmatic. Its task was not to issue infallible definitions or to satisfy a disciple's intellectual curiosity about metaphysical questions. Its sole purpose was to enable people to get across the river of pain to the 'further shore.' His job was to relieve suffering and help his disciples attain the peace of Nibbāṇa. Anything that did not serve that end was of no importance whatsoever.

Hence there were no abstruse theories about the creation of the universe or the existence of a Supreme Being. These matters might be interesting but they would not give a disciple enlightenment or release from *dukkha.* One day, while living in a grove of siṃsāpa trees in Kosambī, the Buddha plucked a few leaves and pointed out to his disciples that there were many more still growing in the wood. So too he had only given them a few teachings and withheld many others. Why? 'Because, my disciples, they will not help you, they are not useful in the quest for holiness, they do not lead to peace and to the direct knowledge of Nibbāṇa.'[5] He told one monk, who kept pestering him about philosophy, that he was like a wounded man who refused to have treatment until he learned the name of the person who had shot him and what village he came from: he would die before he got this useless information. In just the same way, those who refused to live according to the Buddhist method until they knew about the creation of the world or the nature of the Absolute would die in misery before they got an answer to these unknowable questions. What difference did it make if the world was eternal or created in time? Grief, suffering and misery would still exist. The Buddha was concerned simply with the cessation of pain. 'I am preaching a cure for these unhappy conditions here and now,' the Buddha told the philosophically inclined *bhikkhu,* 'so always remember what I have not explained to you and the reason why I have refused to explain it.'[6]

But when he faced his five former companions in the Deer Park, the Buddha had to begin somewhere. How was he going to allay their suspicions? He would have to give some kind of logical explanation of the Four Noble Truths. We do not know what he actually said to the five *bhikkhus* that day. It is most unlikely that the discourse that is called the First Sermon in the

Pāli texts is a verbatim report of his preaching on that occasion. When the scriptures were compiled, the editors probably hit upon this *sutta,* which conveniently sets forth the essentials, and inserted it into the narrative at this point.[7] But in some ways this First Sermon was appropriate. The Buddha was always careful to make his teachings fit the needs of the people he was addressing. These five *bhikkhus* were worried about Gotama's abandonment of asceticism, and so in this *sutta* the Buddha began by reassuring them, explaining the theory behind his Middle Way. People who had 'Gone Forth' into holiness, he said, should avoid the two extremes of sensual pleasure, on the one hand, and excessive mortification on the other. Neither was helpful, because they did not lead to Nibbāṇa. Instead, he had discovered the Eightfold Path, a happy medium between these two alternatives, which, he could guarantee, would lead the monks directly to enlightenment.

Next, the Buddha outlined the Four Noble Truths: the Truth of Suffering, the Truth of the Cause of Suffering, the Truth of the Cessation of Suffering or Nibbāṇa, and the Path that led to this liberation. However, these truths were not presented as metaphysical theories but as a practical program. The word *dhamma* denotes not only what *is,* but what *should* be. The Buddha's Dhamma was a diagnosis of the problem of life and a prescription for cure, which must be followed exactly. Each of the Truths had three components in his sermon. First, he made the *bhikkhus* see the Truth. Next, he explained what had to be done about it: suffering had to be 'fully known'; Craving, the Cause of Suffering, had to be 'given up'; Nibbāṇa, the Cessation of Suffering, had to 'become a reality' in the heart of the Arahant; and the Eightfold Path must be 'followed.' Finally, the Buddha explained what he *had* achieved: he *had* understood *dukkha* 'directly'; he *had* abandoned craving; he *had* experienced Nibbāṇa; he *had* followed the Path to its conclusion. It was, he explained, when he had proved to himself that his Dhamma really worked and that he had actually completed the program, that his enlightenment had been complete: 'I have achieved the final release!' he had cried triumphantly.[8] He had indeed been liberated from *saṃsāra,* he knew that the Middle Way was the true path, and his own life and person proved it.

The Pāli text tells us that as he listened to the Buddha's sermon, Kondañña, one of the five *bhikkhus,* began to experience his teaching 'directly.'[9] It 'rose up' in him, as if from the depths of his own being. It was as though he recognized it – had always known it.[10] This is the way the scriptures always describe a new disciple's conversion to the Dhamma. This was no mere notional assent to a creed. The Buddha was really holding an initiation ceremony in the Deer Park. Like a midwife, he was assisting at the birth of an enlightened human being, or, to use his own metaphor, he was drawing the sword from the scabbard and the snake from its slough. When the gods, who had gathered in the Deer Park to listen to this First Sermon, saw what was happening to Kondañña, they cried out joyfully: 'The Lord has set the Wheel of the Dhamma in motion in the Deer Park of Vārānasī!' The cry was taken up by the gods in one heaven after another, until it reached the abode of Brahma himself. The earth shook and was filled with a light more radiant than any of the gods. 'Kondañña knows! Kondañña knows!' the Buddha exclaimed in delight. Kondañña had become what later Buddhist tradition would call a 'stream-enterer' (*sotāpanna*).[11] He had not yet been fully enlightened, but his doubts had disappeared, he was no longer interested in any other *dhamma,* and he was ready to immerse himself in the Buddha's method, confident that it would carry him forward to Nibbāṇa. He asked to be admitted to the Buddha's Sangha. 'Come, *bhikkhu*,' the Buddha replied. 'The Dhamma has been preached to good effect. Live the holy life that will end your suffering once and for all.'[12]

But the Pāli texts include another version of this first teaching session in the Deer Park. This describes a much longer and quite different process. The Buddha instructed the *bhikkhus* in pairs, while the other three went off to Vārānasī to beg enough food for all six of them. It has been suggested that in these more intimate tutorials, the Buddha was initiating the *bhikkhus* in his special yoga, introducing them to the practice of 'mindfulness' and the 'immeasurables.'[13] Certainly meditation was indispensable to enlightenment. The Dhamma could not become a reality or understood 'directly' unless the aspirants were also sinking deeply into themselves and learning to put their minds and bodies under the Buddha's yogic microscope. Kondañña could not have become a 'stream-enterer' and gained his special 'direct knowledge' of the Dhamma simply by listening to a sermon and accepting its truths on hearsay. The truths of Suffering and Craving could not be properly understood until the *bhikkhus* had become aware of them within the minutiae of their own experience; the Eightfold Path, which he preached, included the discipline of meditation. The instruction of these five *bhikkhus* almost certainly took longer than a single morning; even if they were already accomplished yogins and versed in the ethic of *ahiṃsā*, the Dhamma needed time to take effect. At all events, the Pāli texts tell us, not long after the Dhamma 'rose up' in Kondañña, Vappa, Bhaddiya, Mahānāma and Assaji became 'stream-enterers' too.[14]

The reasoned formulation of the Dhamma was complementary to the practice of meditation, which enabled aspirants to 'realize' it. Through yoga, the *bhikkhus* could identify with the truths that the doctrine tried to express. One of the most frequent subjects of Buddhist meditation was what was called the Chain of Dependent Causation (*Paṭicca-samuppāda*), which the Buddha probably developed at a later stage as a supplement to the Truth of Suffering, even though the Pāli texts say that he was contemplating this Chain immediately before and after his enlightenment.[15] The Chain traces the life cycle of a sentient being through twelve conditioned and conditioning links, illustrating the transitory nature of our lives and showing how each person is perpetually becoming something else.

> On [1] *ignorance* depends [2] *kamma*; on *kamma* depends [3] *consciousness*; on consciousness depends [4] *name and form*; on name and form depend [5] the *sense organs*; on the sense organs depends [6] *contact*; on contact depends [7] *sensation*; on sensation depends [8] *desire*; on desire depends [9] *attachment*; on attachment depends [10] *existence*; on existence depends [11] *birth*; on birth depends [12] *dukkha*: old age and death, sorrow, lamentation, misery, grief and despair.[16]

This Chain became central to Buddhist teaching, but it is not easy to understand. Those who find it somewhat daunting can draw comfort from the fact that the Buddha once rebuked a *bhikkhu* who claimed to find it easy. It should be regarded as a metaphor, which seeks to explain how a person can be reborn when, as the Buddha was beginning to conclude, there was no Self to persist from one life to another. What was it that was born again? Is there a law which links rebirth with *dukkha*?

The terms used in the Chain are rather obscure. 'Name and form,' for example, was simply a Pāli idiom for a 'person'; 'consciousness' (*viññāna*) is not the totality of a person's thoughts and feelings, but a sort of ethereal substance, the last idea or impulse of a dying human being, which has been conditioned by all the *kamma* of his or her life. This 'consciousness' becomes the germ of a new 'name and form' in the womb of its mother. The personality of this embryo is conditioned by the quality of the dying 'consciousness' of its predecessor. Once the fetus is linked with this 'consciousness,' a new life cycle can begin. The embryo develops sense organs and, after its birth, these make 'contact' with the external world. This sensual contact gives rise to 'sensations' or feelings, which lead to 'desire,' the most powerful cause of *dukkha.* Desire leads to 'attachments' which prevent our liberation and enlightenment, and which doom us to a new 'existence,' a new birth and further sorrow, sickness, grief and death.[17]

The Chain begins with ignorance, which thus becomes the ultimate if not the most powerful cause of suffering. Most of the monks in the Ganges region believed that desire was the first cause of *dukkha,* while the *Upaniṣads* and Sāṃkhya thought that ignorance of the nature of reality was the main bar to liberation. The Buddha was able to combine these two causes.[18] He believed that each person is alive because he or she was preceded in a former existence by beings who did not know the Four Truths and could not, therefore, extricate themselves from Craving and Suffering. A person who was not correctly informed could make serious practical mistakes. A yogin might imagine, for example, that one of the higher states of trance was Nibbāṇa and would not make the extra effort to achieve complete release. In most versions of the Chain given in the Pāli texts, the second link is not *kamma* but the more difficult term *sankhāra* (formation). But the two words both derive from the same verbal root: *kr* (to do). *Sankhāra* has been somewhat clumsily translated: 'states or things being formed or prepared.'[19] Thus our deeds (*kamma*) are preparing the 'consciousness' for a future existence; they are forming and conditioning it. Since the Buddha saw our intentions as mental *kamma,* the Chain points out that those emotions which motivate our external actions will have future consequences; a lifetime of greedy, deluded choices will affect the quality of our last, dying thought (*viññāna*) and this will affect the kind of life we have next time. Was this final, dying 'consciousness' that passes into a new 'name and form' an eternal, constant entity? Would the same person live again and again? Yes and no. The Buddha did not believe that 'consciousness' was the kind of permanent, eternal Self sought by the yogins, but saw it as a last flickering energy, like a flame that leaps from one wick to another.[20] A flame is never constant; a fire which is lit at nightfall both is and is not the fire that is still burning at daybreak.

There are no fixed entities in the Chain. Each link depends upon another and leads directly to something else. It is a perfect expression of the 'becoming' which the Buddha saw as an inescapable fact of human life. We are always trying to become something different, striving for a new mode of being, and indeed cannot remain in one state for long. Each *sankhāra* gives place to the next; each state is simply the prelude to another. Nothing in life can, therefore, be regarded as stable. A person should be regarded as a process, not an unchangeable entity. When a *bhikkhu* meditated on the Chain and saw it yogically, becoming mindful of the way each thought and sensation rose and fell away, he acquired a 'direct knowledge' of the Truth that nothing could be relied upon, that everything was impermanent (*anicca*), and would be inspired to redouble his efforts to extricate himself from this endless Chain of cause and effect.[21]

This constant self-appraisal and attention to the fluctuations of everyday life induced a state of calm control. When the daily practice of mindfulness was continued in his meditations, it brought the *bhikkhu* an insight into the nature of personality that was more deeply rooted and immediate than any that could be produced by rational deduction. It also led to greater self-discipline. The Buddha had no time for the ecstatic trances of the *brahmins.* He insisted that his monks should always conduct themselves with sobriety, and forbade emotional display. But mindfulness also made the *bhikkhu* more aware of the morality of his behavior. He noticed how his own 'unskillful' actions could harm other people and that even his motivation could be injurious. So, the Buddha concluded, our intentions were *kamma* and had consequences.[22] The intentions, conscious or unconscious, that inspired our actions were mental acts that were just as important as any external deeds. This redefinition of *kamma* as *cetanā* (intention; choice) was revolutionary; it deepened the entire question of morality, which was now located in the mind and heart and could not merely be a matter of outward behavior.

But mindfulness (*sati*) led the Buddha to a still more radical conclusion. Three days after the five *bhikkhus* had become 'stream-enterers,' the Buddha delivered a second sermon in the Deer Park, in which he expounded his unique doctrine of *anattā* (no-self).[23] He divided the human personality into five 'heaps' or 'constituents' (*khandhas*): the body, feelings, perceptions, volitions (conscious and unconscious) and consciousness, and asked the *bhikkhus* to consider each *khandha* in turn. The body or our feelings, for example, constantly changed from one moment to the next. They caused us pain, let us down and frustrated us. The same had to be said of our perceptions and volitions. Thus each *khandha,* subject as it was to *dukkha,* flawed and transitory, could not constitute or include the Self sought by so many of the ascetics and yogins. Was it not true, the Buddha asked his disciples, that after examining each *khandha,* an honest person found that he could not wholly identify with it, because it was so unsatisfactory? He was bound to say, 'This is not mine; this is not what I really am; this is not my self.'[24] But the Buddha did not simply deny the existence of the eternal, absolute Self. He now claimed that there was no stable, lower-case self either. The terms 'self' and 'myself' were simply conventions. The personality had no fixed or changeless core. As the Chain showed, every sentient being was in a state of constant flux; he or she was merely a succession of temporary, mutable states of existence.

The Buddha pressed this message home throughout his life. Where the seventeenth-century French philosopher René Descartes would declare 'I think, therefore I am,' the Buddha came to the opposite conclusion. The more he thought, in the mindful, yogic way he had developed, the clearer it seemed that what we call the 'self' is a delusion. In his view, the more closely we examine ourselves, the harder it becomes to find anything that we can pinpoint as a fixed entity. The human personality was not a static being to which things happened. Put under the microscope of yogic analysis, each person was a process. The Buddha liked to use such metaphors as a blazing fire or a rushing stream to describe the personality; it had some kind of identity, but was never the same from one moment to another. At each second, a fire was different; it had consumed and re-created itself, just as people did. In a particularly vivid simile, the Buddha compared the human mind to a monkey ranging through the forest: 'it grabs one branch, and then, letting that go, seizes another.'[25] What we experience as the 'self' is really just a convenience-term, because we are constantly changing. In the same way, milk can become, successively, curds, butter, ghee, and fine-extract of ghee. There is no point in calling any one of these transformations 'milk,' even though there is a sense in which it is correct to do so.[26]

The eighteenth-century Scottish empiricist David Hume came to a similar conclusion, but with an important difference: he did not expect his insight to affect the moral conduct of his readers. But in Axial Age India, knowledge had no significance unless it was found to be transformative. A *dhamma* was an imperative to action, and the doctrine of *anattā* was not an abstract philosophical proposition but required Buddhists to *behave* as though the ego did not exist. The ethical effects of this are far-reaching. Not only does the idea of 'self' lead to unskillful thoughts about 'me and mine' and inspire our selfish cravings; egotism can arguably be described as the source of all evil: an excessive attachment to the self can lead to envy or hatred of rivals, conceit, megalomania, pride, cruelty, and, when the self feels threatened, to violence and the destruction of others. Western people often regard the Buddha's doctrine of *anattā* as nihilistic and depressing, but at their best all the great world religions formed during the Axial Age seek to curb the voracious, frightened ego that does so much harm. The Buddha, however, was more radical. His teaching of *anattā* did not seek to annihilate the self. He simply denied that the self had ever existed. It was a mistake to think of it as a constant reality. Any such misconception was a symptom of that ignorance which kept us bound to the cycle of suffering.

Anattā, like any Buddhist teaching, was not a philosophical doctrine but was primarily pragmatic. Once a disciple had acquired, through yoga and mindfulness, a 'direct' knowledge of *anattā*, he would be delivered from the pains and perils of egotism, which would become a logical impossibility. In the Axial countries, we have seen that people felt suddenly alone and lost in the world, in exile from Eden and the sacred dimension that gives life meaning and value. Much of their pain sprang from insecurity in a world of heightened individualism in the new market economy. The Buddha tried to make his *bhikkhus* see that they did not have a 'self' that needed to be defended, inflated, flattered, cajoled and enhanced at the expense of others. Once a monk had become practiced in the discipline of mindfulness, he would see how ephemeral what we call the 'self' really was. He would no longer introject his ego into these passing mental states and identify with them. He would learn to regard his desires, fears and cravings as remote phenomena that had little to do with him. Once he had attained this dispassion and equanimity, the Buddha explained to the five *bhikkhus* at the end of his Second Sermon, he would find that he was ripe for enlightenment. 'His greed fades away, and once his cravings disappear, he experiences the release of his heart.' He had achieved his goal and could utter the same triumphant cry as the Buddha himself, when he had attained enlightenment. 'The holy life has been lived out to its conclusion! What had to be done has been accomplished; there is nothing else to do!'[27]

And, indeed, it was when they heard the Buddha explaining *anattā* that all five *bhikkhus* attained their full enlightenment and became Arahants. The texts tell us that this teaching filled their hearts with joy.[28] This might seem strange: why should they be so happy to hear that the self that we all cherish does not exist? The Buddha knew that *anattā* could be frightening. An outsider, hearing the doctrine for the first time, might panic, thinking: 'I am going to be annihilated and destroyed; I will no longer exist!'[29] But the Pāli texts show that people accepted *anattā* with enormous relief and delight, as the five *bhikkhus* did, and this, as it were, 'proved' that it was true. When people lived as though the ego did not exist, they found that they were happier. They experienced the same kind of enlargement of being as came from a practice of the 'immeasurables,' which were designed to dethrone the self from the center of our private universe and put other beings in its place. Egotism is constricting; when we see things only from a selfish point of view, our vision is limited. To live beyond the reach of greed, hatred, and the fears that come with an acute anxiety about our status and survival is liberating. *Anattā* may sound bleak when proposed as an abstract idea, but when it was lived out it transformed people's lives. By living *as though* they had no self, people found that they had conquered their egotism and felt a great deal better. By understanding *anattā* with the 'direct knowledge' of a yogin, they found that they had crossed over into a richer, fuller existence. *Anattā* must, therefore, tell us something true about the human condition, even though we cannot prove empirically that the self does not exist.

The Buddha believed that a selfless life would introduce men and women to Nibbāṇa. Monotheists would say that it would bring them into the presence of God. But the Buddha found the notion of a personalized deity too limiting, because it suggested that the supreme Truth was only another being. Nibbāṇa was neither a personality nor a place like Heaven. The Buddha always denied the existence of any absolute principle or Supreme Being, since this could be another thing to cling to, another fetter and impediment to enlightenment. Like the doctrine of the Self, the notion of God can also be used to prop up and inflate the ego. The most sensitive monotheists in Judaism, Christianity and Islam would all be aware of this danger and would speak of God in ways that are reminiscent of the Buddha's reticence about Nibbāṇa. They would also insist that God was not another being, that our notion of 'existence' was so limited that it was more accurate to say that God did not exist and that 'he' was Nothing. But on a more popular level, it is certainly true that 'God' is often reduced to an idol created in the image and likeness of 'his' worshippers. If we imagine God to be a being like ourselves writ large, with likes and dislikes similar to our own, it is all too easy to make 'him' endorse some of our most uncharitable, selfish and even lethal hopes, fears and prejudices. This limited God has thus contributed to some of the worst religious atrocities in history. The Buddha would have described belief in a deity who gives a seal of sacred approval to our own selves as 'unskillful': it could only embed the believer in the damaging and dangerous egotism that he or she was supposed to transcend. Enlightenment demands that we reject any such false prop. It seems that a 'direct' yogic understanding of *anattā* was one of the chief ways in which the early Buddhists experienced Nibbāṇa. And, indeed, the Axial Age faiths all insist in one way or another that we will only fulfil ourselves if we practice total self-abandonment. To go into religion to 'get' something, such as a comfortable retirement in the afterlife, is to miss the point. The five *bhikkhus* who attained enlightenment in the Deer Park had understood this at a profound level.

Now they had to bring the Dhamma to others. As the Buddha himself had learned, an understanding of the First

Noble Truth of *dukkha* meant empathizing with the sorrow of others; the doctrine of *anattā* implied that an enlightened person must live not for her- or himself but for others. There were now six Arahants, but they were still too few to bring light to a world engulfed in pain. Then, seemingly out of the blue, the Buddha's little *sangha* got an influx of new members. The first was Yasa, the son of a rich merchant of Vārānasī. Like the young Gotama he had lived in the lap of luxury, but one night he awoke to find his servants lying asleep all round his bed, looking so ugly and unseemly that he was filled with disgust. The fact that other texts, such as the *Nidāna Kathā*, would later, without apology, tell exactly the same tale about the young Gotama shows the archetypal nature of the story. It was a stylized way of describing the alienation that so many people in the Ganges region were experiencing. The Pāli story tells us that Yasa felt sick at heart and that he cried in distress: 'This is terrifying! Horrible!' The world seemed suddenly profane, meaningless and, therefore, unbearable. At once, Yasa decided to 'Go Forth' and seek something better. He slipped on a pair of gold slippers, crept out of his father's house, and made his way to the Deer Park, still muttering: 'Terrifying! Horrible!' Then he came upon the Buddha, who had risen early and was enjoying a walk in the cool light of dawn. With the enhanced mental power of an enlightened man, the Buddha recognized Yasa, and motioned him to a seat, saying with a smile: 'It is not terrifying; it is not horrible. Come and sit down, Yasa, and I will teach you the Dhamma.'[30]

The Buddha's serenity and gentleness reassured Yasa at once. He no longer felt that sickening dread, but was happy and hopeful. With his heart joyful and at peace, he was in exactly the right mood for enlightenment. He took off his slippers and sat down beside the Buddha, who instructed him in the Middle Way, step by step, beginning with very basic teaching about the importance of avoiding *tanhā* and sensual pleasure, and describing the benefits of the holy life. But when he saw that Yasa was receptive and ready, he went on to teach him the Four Noble Truths. As Yasa listened, 'the pure vision of the Dhamma rose up in him,' and the truths sank into his soul, as easily, we are told, as a dye penetrates and colors a clean piece of cloth.[31] Once Yasa's mind had been 'dyed' by the Dhamma, there was no way of separating the two. This was 'direct knowledge,' because Yasa had experienced the Dhamma at such a profound level that he had wholly identified with it. It had transformed him and 'dyed' his entire being. This would be a common experience when people heard the Dhamma for the first time, especially when instructed by the Buddha himself. They felt that the Dhamma fit their needs perfectly, that it was entirely natural and congenial to them, and that, in some sense, they had always known it. We do not find in the Pāli texts any agonized or dramatic conversions, similar to St. Paul's on the road to Damascus. Any such wrenching experience would have been regarded by the Buddha as 'unskillful.' People must be in tune with their natures, as he himself had been under the rose-apple tree.

Just as Yasa had become a 'stream-enterer,' the Buddha noticed an older merchant coming toward them and realized that this must be Yasa's father; he then had recourse to the *iddhi* or spiritual powers that were thought to come with advanced proficiency in yoga, and made Yasa disappear. Yasa's father was greatly distressed; the whole household was searching for Yasa, but he had followed the print of the golden slippers which brought him directly to the Buddha. Again, the Buddha made the merchant sit down, hinting that he would see Yasa very soon, and instructed the father as he had the son. The merchant was immediately impressed: 'Lord, that is superb! Quite superb!' he cried. 'The Dhamma has been made so clear that it is as though you are holding up a lamp in the darkness and putting right something that has gone profoundly wrong.' He was then the first to make what has since become known as the Triple Refuge: an assertion of complete confidence in the Buddha, the Dhamma, and the Sangha of *bhikkhus*.[32] He also became one of the first lay followers, who continued to live as a householder but practiced a modified form of the Buddhist method.

As Yasa, unseen by his father, listened to the Buddha, he attained full enlightenment and entered into Nibbāṇa. At this point, the Buddha revealed him to his father, and the merchant begged Yasa to return home, if only for his mother's sake. The Buddha, however, gently explained that Yasa had become an Arahant and would now find it impossible to live the life of a householder. He was no longer afflicted by the cravings and desires that would enable him to fulfill a householder's reproductive and economic duties; he would require hours of silence and privacy for meditation that would not be possible in a family home. He could not return. Yasa's father understood, but begged the Buddha to dine at his house that day, with Yasa as his attendant monk. During the meal, the Buddha instructed Yasa's mother and his former wife, and they became the Buddha's first women lay disciples.

But the news spread beyond the household. Four of Yasa's friends, who came from Vārānasī's leading merchant families, were so impressed when they heard that he was now wearing the yellow robe that they came to the Buddha for instruction. So did fifty of Yasa's friends from *brahmin* and *ksatriya* families in the surrounding countryside. All these young men from the noble and aristocratic castes soon achieved enlightenment, so that in a very short space of time, there were, the texts tell us, sixty-one Arahants in the world, including the Buddha himself.

The Sangha was becoming a sizeable sect, but the new Arahants could not be allowed to luxuriate in their newfound liberation. Their vocation was not a selfish retreat from the world; they too had to return to the marketplace to help others find release from pain. They would now live for others, as the Dhamma enjoined. 'Go now,' the Buddha told his sixty *bhikkhus*,

> and travel for the welfare and happiness of the people, out of compassion for the world, for the benefit, welfare and happiness of gods and men. No two of you go the same way. Teach the Dhamma, *bhikkhus*, and meditate on the holy life. There are beings with only a little desire left within them who are languishing for lack of hearing the Dhamma; they will understand it.[33]

Buddhism was not a doctrine for a privileged elite; it was a religion for 'the people,' for 'the many (*bahujana*).' In practice, it appealed mostly to the upper classes and to intellectuals, but in principle it was open to anybody, and nobody, whatever his or her caste, was excluded. For the first time in history, somebody had envisaged a religious program that was not confined to a single group, but was intended for the whole of humanity. This was no esoteric truth, like that preached by the sages of the *Upaniṣads.* It was out in the open, in the towns, the new cities and along the trade routes. Whenever they heard the Dhamma, people started to throng into the Sangha, which became a force to be reckoned with in the Ganges plain. The members of the new Order were known as 'The Ordained Followers of the Teacher from Sakka,' but they called themselves simply the Union of *Bhikkhus* (*Bhikkhu-Sangha*).[34] People who joined found that they had 'woken up' to whole regions of their humanity which had hitherto lain dormant; a new social and religious reality had come into being.

5 MISSION

BUDDHIST ART USUALLY depicts the Buddha sitting alone, lost in solitary meditation, but in fact the greater part of his life, once he had begun to preach the Dhamma, was spent surrounded by large, noisy crowds of people. When he traveled, he was usually accompanied by hundreds of *bhikkhus*, who tended to chatter so loudly that occasionally the Buddha had to plead for a little quiet. His lay disciples often followed the procession of monks along the roads, in chariots and wagons loaded with provisions. The Buddha lived in towns and cities, not in remote forest hermitages. But even though the last forty-five years of his life were passed in the public eye, the texts treat this long and important phase rather perfunctorily, leaving the biographer little to work with. It is quite the opposite with Jesus. The Gospels tell us next to nothing about Jesus's early life and only seriously begin their story when he starts his preaching mission. The Buddhist scriptures, however, record the Buddha's sermons and describe the first five years of his teaching career in some detail, but after that the Buddha fades from view and the last twenty years of his life are almost entirely unrecorded.

The Buddha would have approved of this reticence. The

last thing he wanted was a personality cult, and he always insisted that it was the Dhamma and not himself that was important. As we have noted, he used to say, 'He who sees me sees the Dhamma, and he who sees the Dhamma sees me.'[1] Furthermore, after his enlightenment nothing else could really happen to him. He had no 'self,' his egotism had been extinguished, and he was known as the Tathāgata, one who had, quite simply, 'gone.' Even when the Pāli texts do recount the early years of his mission, they are less interested in historical fact and more interested in the symbolic meaning of their stories. The Buddha had become an archetype of the spiritual life, an embodiment of the Dhamma and of Nibbāṇa. He was a new kind of human being: no longer caught in the toils of greed and hatred, he had learned to manipulate his psyche in order to live without egotism. He was still living in the world, but inhabited another sacred dimension, too, which monotheists would call the divine presence. In their account of these first teaching years, the texts tell us nothing about the Buddha's thoughts and feelings, therefore, but use his activities to show how the early Buddhists related to the urban, commercial, political and religious world of north India.

The scriptures say that the Buddha attained Nibbāṇa in late April or early May, but they do not reveal the year in which this important event took place. The conventional date has long been held to be 528 B.C.E., though some modern scholarship would put it as late as 450.[2] If we follow the possibly accelerated chronology of the Pāli texts, the Buddha might have sent the sixty monks out to teach in September, after the end of the monsoon. Like the other *sanghas*, the Buddha's new Order was a loose, peripatetic organization. The monks slept rough, wherever they could: 'in the woods, in the roots of trees, under overhanging rocks, in ravines, in hillside caves, in cemeteries, in jungle groves, in the open, on heaps of straw.'[3] But every day they spent time in meditation and preached to the people who needed the Dhamma, especially those who lived in the new cities where the malaise of the time was most acutely felt. Their preaching was successful: they not only attracted lay disciples but new recruits to the Sangha, and the Buddha authorized the sixty to receive novices themselves and ordain them as fully fledged monks.[4]

Left to himself once more, the Buddha returned to Uruvelā. On his way, he preached the Dhamma to thirty rowdy young men in hot pursuit of a local courtesan, who had decamped with their money. 'Which is better for you?' the Buddha asked. 'To look for a woman or to find yourselves?'[5] The incident was a graphic allegory of humanity's pointless stampede after pleasure, which can only frustrate and impoverish. After listening to the Buddha, the youths all became 'stream-enterers' and joined the Sangha. But when he reached Uruvelā, the Buddha achieved a far more startling conversion, when he successfully initiated a whole *sangha* of one thousand *brahmins,* who were living in the forests around Uruvelā, Gayā and beside the river Nerañjarā, under the leadership of the three Kassapa brothers. This tale should probably be read as a parable, depicting the early Buddhists' confrontation with the old Vedic tradition.[6] These *brahmins* had 'Gone Forth' and let their hair grow wild and matted as a sign of their repudiation of the settled, ordered lifestyle of normal society, but they still observed the old rites scrupulously and tended the three sacred fires.

The Buddha spent the winter with the Uruvelā community and worked a number of impressive miracles. He tamed a highly dangerous cobra, a popular symbol of the divine, which the *brahmins* housed in their sacred fire chamber. He entertained gods, who visited his hermitage at night and lit the whole wood with unearthly radiance. He split logs miraculously for the fire ceremonies, ascended to the heavens and brought back a celestial flower, and showed the Kassapa who was leader of the Uruvelā group that he could read his mind. Both the Pāli texts and the later biographies contain stories of such signs and wonders performed by the Buddha, which is, at first glance, surprising. The practice of yoga was thought to give a skilled yogin powers (*iddhi*), which showed the dominion of a trained mind over matter, but yogins generally warned against the exercise of *iddhi*, because it was all too easy for a spiritual man to degenerate into a mere magician.[7] The Buddha himself was highly critical of such exhibitionism, and forbade his disciples to exercise *iddhi* in public. But the monks who composed the Pāli texts would have believed that such feats were possible, and they probably used these tales as a polemic. In their preaching, the Theravādin monks who composed these texts may have found it useful to relate that the Buddha had these impressive powers. Further, when disputing with *brahmins* and officials of Vedic religion, it was helpful to be able to relate that the Buddha had taken on the old gods (like the sacred cobra in the fire chamber) and soundly defeated them; even though he was a mere *ksatriya*, he had more power than did *brahmins*. Later the texts tell us that the Buddha challenged the whole caste system: 'It is not simply birth that makes a person a *brahmin* or an outcaste,' he insisted, 'but our actions (*kamma*).'[8] Religious status depended on moral behavior, not upon the accident of heredity. As always, the Buddha, like the other great Axial sages, argued that faith must be informed by ethics, without which ritual was useless.

It was morality, not the exercise of the Buddha's miraculous powers, which finally convinced Kassapa. Here again, the texts may also have been suggesting that a showy display of *iddhi* could be counterproductive: it certainly did not convince a skeptic. After each miracle, Kassapa merely said to himself: 'This great monk is impressive and powerful, but he is not an Arahant like me.' Eventually, the Buddha shocked him out of his pride and complacency. 'Kassapa,' he said, 'you are not an Arahant, and if you continue like this, you will never achieve enlightenment.' Such rampant egotism was quite incompatible with the spiritual life. The rebuke hit home. As a famous ascetic, Kassapa would have known all about the dangers of such self-esteem. He prostrated himself on the ground and begged for admission to the Sangha. He was followed by both his brothers and all their thousand disciples. There were now a host of new novices, who shaved off their matted locks, threw away their sacred utensils, and became 'stream-enterers.'[9] Then they all gathered together at Gayā to hear the Buddha's third great sermon.

'*Bhikkhus,*' the Buddha began, 'everything is burning.' The senses and everything that they feed upon in the external world, the body, the mind and the emotions were all ablaze. What caused this conflagration? The three fires of greed, hatred and delusion.[10] As long as people fed these flames, they would continue to burn and could never reach the coolness of Nibbāṇa. The five *khandha* (the 'heaps' or 'constituents' of the personality) were thus tacitly compared to 'bundles' of firewood. There was a pun also in the word *upādāna* ('clinging'), whose root meaning is 'fuel.'[11] It was our grasping desire for the things of this world which kept us ablaze and impeded our enlightenment. As always, this greed and craving was coupled with the hatred which is responsible for so much of the evil and violence in the world. As long as the third fire of ignorance continued to rage, a person could not realize the Four Noble Truths, which were essential for release from the smoldering cycle of 'birth, old age and death, with sorrow, mourning, pain, grief and despair.'[12] A *bhikkhu* must, therefore, become dispassionate. The art of mindfulness would teach him to become detached from his five *khandha* and douse the flames. Then he would experience the liberation and peace of Nibbāṇa.

The Fire Sermon was a brilliant critique of the Vedic system. Its sacred symbol, fire, was an image of everything the Buddha felt to be wrong with life: it represented the hearth and home from which all earnest seekers must 'Go Forth,' and was an eloquent emblem of the restless, destructive but transient forces that make up human consciousness. The three fires of greed, hatred and ignorance were an ironic counterpart to the three holy fires of the Vedas: by tending these in the mistaken belief that they formed a priestly elite, the *brahmins* were simply fueling their own egotism. The sermon was also an illustration of the Buddha's skill in adapting his Dhamma to his audience, so that he could truly speak to their condition. After the former fire-worshippers had listened to the Buddha's sermon, which spoke so powerfully to their religious consciousness, they all achieved Nibbāṇa and became Arahants.

In late December, the Buddha set out for Rājagaha, the capital of Magadha, accompanied by these thousand new *bhikkhus.* Their arrival caused a stir. People in the cities were hungry for new spirituality, and as soon as King Bimbisāra heard that a man who claimed to be a Buddha was encamped outside the city in the Sapling Grove, he went to visit him with a huge entourage of *brahmin* householders. They were all astonished to find that Kassapa, the former head of the Uruvelā community, was now the Buddha's disciple, and were greatly impressed when Kassapa explained to them the reasons why he had abandoned fire-worship. When they heard the Buddha preach, all the householders – the Pāli text tells us that there were 120,000 of them – became lay followers, and last of all, King Bimbisāra prostrated himself before the Buddha and begged to be received as a lay disciple too. Ever since he was a boy, the king had hoped to listen to a Buddha preaching a Dhamma that he could understand. Now his wish had been granted. It was the start of a long partnership between the Buddha and the king, who invited him to dinner that night.

During the meal, the king gave the Sangha a gift that would have a decisive influence on the development of the Buddhist Order. He donated a pleasure-park (*ārāma*) known as the Bamboo Grove of Veluvana, just outside Rājagaha, as a home for the Sangha of Bhikkhus. The monks could live there in a quiet, peaceful place that was at the same time accessible to the city and to the people who would need to consult them. The Grove was neither 'too far from the town, nor too near... accessible to the people, but peaceful, and secluded.'[13] The Buddha accepted the gift, which was a perfect solution. The 'seclusion' of his monks was to be a psychological one, not a total physical segregation from the world. The Order existed for the people, not simply for the monks' personal sanctification. The *bhikkhus* would need a degree of quiet for meditation, where they could develop the dispassion and internal solitude that led to Nibbāṇa, but if they were to live entirely for others, as the Dhamma demanded, lay folk must be able to visit them and learn how to assuage their own suffering. The gift of the Bamboo Grove set a precedent, and wealthy donors often gave the Sangha similar parks in the suburbs, which became the regional headquarters of the wandering *bhikkhus.*

The Buddha remained in the new *ārāma* for two months, and it was during this time that his two most important disciples joined the Sangha. Sāriputta and Moggallāna had both been born to *brahmin* families in small villages outside Rājagaha. They renounced the world on the same day, and joined the *sangha* of the Skeptics, led by Sañjaya. But neither attained full enlightenment, and they made a pact that whichever of them achieved Nibbāṇa first would tell the other immediately. At the time of the Buddha's visit the two friends were living in Rājagaha, and one day Sāriputta saw Assaji (one of the original five *bhikkhus*) begging for alms. He was at once struck by the serenity and poise of the monk and was convinced that this man had found a spiritual solution, so he hailed him in the traditional way, asking Assaji which teacher and *dhamma* he followed. Pleading that he was a mere beginner in the holy life, Assaji gave only a brief summary of the Dhamma, but that was enough. Sāriputta became a 'stream-enterer' on the spot, and hurried to tell Moggallāna the news. His friend also became a 'stream-enterer,' and they went together to the Bamboo Grove to ask the Buddha for admission to the Sangha, taking, to Sañjaya's chagrin, 250 of his disciples with them. When the Buddha saw Sāriputta and Moggallāna approaching, he instinctively knew how gifted they were. 'These will be my chief disciples,' he told the *bhikkhus.* 'They will do great things for the Sangha.'[14] And so it proved. The two friends became the inspiration for the two main schools of Buddhism that developed some 200 to 300 years after the Buddha's death.[15] The more austere and monastically inclined Theravāda regard Sāriputta as a second founder. He was of an analytical cast of mind and could express the Dhamma in a way that was easy to memorize. But his piety was too dry for the more populist Mahāyāna school, whose version of Buddhism is more democratic and emphasizes the importance of compassion. The Mahāyāna has taken Moggallāna as their mentor; he was known for his *iddhi*, would ascend mystically to the heavens and, through his yogic powers, had an uncanny ability to read people's minds. The fact that the Buddha praised both Sāriputta and Moggallāna shows that both schools are regarded as authentic, and indeed they have coexisted more peacefully than, for example, Catholics and Protestants have in the Christian world.

Not everybody was enamored of the Buddha, however. During his stay in the Bamboo Grove, many of the citizens of Rājagaha were understandably worried about the dramatic growth of the Sangha. First the wild-haired *brahmins*, now Sañjaya's Skeptics – who would be next? By taking away all the young men, the monk Gotama was making them all childless and turning their women into widows. Soon their families would die out! But when this was brought to the Buddha's attention, he told the *bhikkhus* not to worry; this was only a seven-day wonder, and, sure enough, after a week or so the trouble stopped.[16]

At about this time, the Pāli texts tell us, the Buddha made a visit to his father's house in Kapilavatthu – but they give us no details. The later scriptures and commentaries, however, flesh out the bare bones of the Pāli text, and these post-canonical tales have become part of the Buddha's legend.[17] They tell us that Suddhodana heard that his son, now a famous Buddha, was preaching in Rājagaha, and sent a messenger to him, with a huge entourage, to invite him to pay a visit to Kapilavatthu.

But when this crowd of Sakyans heard the Buddha preach, they all became Arahants and forgot Suddhodana's message – a sequence of events that happened nine times. Finally, the invitation was passed on to the Buddha, who set out for his home town with twenty thousand *bhikkhus*. The Sakyans put the Nigrodha Park outside Kapilavatthu at the *bhikkhus'* disposal, and this became the Sangha's chief headquarters in Sakka, but, showing the pride and hauteur for which they were famous, the Sakyans refused to pay homage to the Buddha. So, descending, as it were, to their level, the Buddha staged a striking display of *iddhi*. He levitated, jets of fire and water gushed from his limbs, and finally he walked along a jeweled causeway in the sky. Perhaps he was trying, as was his wont, to speak to the Sakyans in a way that they could understand and enter into their mind-set. His father Suddhodana had wanted him to be a *cakkavatti*, a World Ruler, and this legendary figure, it was said, would also stride majestically through the skies. In Uruvelā, the Buddha had shown the *brahmin* ascetics that he could overcome their gods; now he showed the Sakyans that he was more than equal to any *cakkavatti*. And the spectacle had an effect, though a superficial one. The Sakyans were stunned into acquiescence and bowed down before the Buddha.

But, as usual, *iddhi* could not achieve a lasting result. The next day, Suddhodana was scandalized to see his son begging for food in Kapilavatthu: how dared he bring the family name into such disrepute! But the Buddha sat his father down and explained the Dhamma to him, and Suddhodana's heart softened. He immediately became a 'stream-enterer,' even though he did not request ordination in the Sangha. He took the Buddha's bowl from him and led him into the house, where, during the meal that was prepared in his honor, all the women of the household became lay disciples, with one notable exception. The Buddha's former wife remained aloof, still, perhaps understandably, hostile to the man who had abandoned her without saying good-bye.

The Pāli texts record that at some unspecified time after this visit to Kapilavatthu, some of the leading youths of Sakka made the Going Forth and joined the Sangha, including the Buddha's seven-year-old son Rāhula, who had to wait until he was twenty before he was ordained, and three of the Buddha's kinsfolk: his cousin, Ānanda; his half-brother, Nanda; and Devadatta, his brother-in-law. They were accompanied by their barber, Upāli, who had been taken along to shave the new *bhikkhus'* heads, but asked for admission himself. His companions asked that the barber be admitted before them, to humble their Sakyan pride.[18] Some of these Sakyans became notable figures in the Order. Upāli became the leading expert in the rule of the monastic life, and Ānanda, a gentle, scrupulous man, became the Buddha's personal attendant during his last twenty years. Because Ānanda was closer to the Buddha than anybody else and was with him almost all of the time, he became extremely knowledgeable about the Buddha's sermons and sayings, but he was not a skilled yogin. Despite the fact that he became the most learned authority on the Dhamma, without the ability to meditate, he did not attain Nibbāṇa during the Buddha's lifetime. As for Devadatta, the scriptures, we shall see, assign him a role that is similar to that of Judas in the Gospel story.

The mention of the Gospels, with their colorful portraits of Jesus's disciples, makes a Western reader long to know more about these early Buddhists. Who were these people who flocked into the Sangha by the thousand? What drew them to the Buddha? The Pāli texts tell us little. The legends indicate that the first recruits came from the *brahmin* and *ksatriya* castes, though the message was preached to 'the many,' and everybody was welcome to join. Merchants were also attracted to the Order; like the monks, they were the 'new men' of the developing society, and needed a faith that reflected their essentially casteless status. But there are no detailed stories of individual conversions, such as the Gospel tales of fishermen dropping their nets and tax collectors leaving their counting houses. Ānanda and Devadatta stand out from the crowd of *bhikkhus,* but their portraits are still emblematic and stylized compared with the more vivid character studies of some of Jesus's disciples. Even Sāriputta and Mogallāna, the leading disciples of the Buddha, are presented as colorless figures with apparently little personality. There are no touching vignettes about the Buddha's relationship with his son: Rāhula appears in the Pāli legends simply as another monk. The Buddha instructs him in meditation, as he would any other *bhikkhu,* and there is nothing in the narrative to suggest that they are father and son. We are left with images, not with personalities, and with our Western love of individuality, we can feel dissatisfied.

But this is to misunderstand the nature of the Buddhist experience. Many of these early monks achieved enlightenment precisely by contemplating the doctrine of *anattā.* This enabled them to transcend self; indeed, the Buddha denied that there was any such thing as a constant personality. He would have regarded the obstinate belief in a sacred, irreducible nub of selfhood as an 'unskillful' delusion that would get in the way of enlightenment. As a result of the spirituality of *anattā,* the Buddha himself is presented in the Pāli Canon as a type rather than an individual. He contends with other types: with Skeptics, *brahmins* and Jains. He owed his liberation precisely to the extinction of the unique traits and idiosyncrasies that Western people prize in their heroes. The same goes for his disciples. There is little to distinguish the Buddha from his *bhikkhus*, who are all depicted as minor Buddhas. Like him, they have become impersonal and have vanished as individuals. The Canonical texts preserve this anonymity by declining to delve into the secrets of their hearts. Nor will they reveal the lovable quirks in their characters before the achievement of enlightenment. It may be no accident that it is Devadatta and Ānanda who stand out from the rank and file. Devadatta is filled with egotism, and the gentle Ānanda has failed to achieve enlightenment and consequently has more observable personal traits than, say, a spiritual giant like Sāriputta. We see farther into Ānanda's heart during the last days of the Buddha's life, but, as we shall see, he cannot share the Buddha's perspective. To a Westerner, who would decry this loss of personality, the *bhikkhus* would probably reply that the surrender of the ego was a price worth paying for the inner peace of Nibbāṇa, which is probably impossible for anybody who is still immured in selfhood.

But the impersonality of the Buddha and his disciples did not mean that they were cold and unfeeling. They were not only gentle and compassionate, but deeply sociable, and their attempt to reach out to 'the many' attracted people who found this lack of egotism compelling.

Like all his monks, the Buddha was constantly on the road, preaching to as wide an audience as possible, but during the three months of the monsoon, when travel was difficult, he took to staying in the Bamboo Grove outside Rājagaha. Even though the park now belonged to the Sangha, the *bhikkhus* had not built in it, but still lived in the open. A rich merchant, however, visited the Grove, liked what he saw, and offered to build sixty huts for the monks, and the Buddha gave his permission. The merchant then invited the Buddha and his monks to a meal. It was no small matter to feed such a large gathering, and on the morning of the dinner, the household was in an uproar as the servants prepared a delicious meal of broth, rice, sauces, and sweets. The merchant was so busy hurrying about and giving orders that he scarcely had time to greet his brother-in-law, Anāthapindika, a merchant from Sāvatthī, who had come to Rājagaha on business. 'Whatever is going on?' Anāthapindika asked in bewilderment. Usually when he visited the household his brother-in-law could not do enough for him. Was there a wedding? Or was the family about to entertain King Bimbisāra? 'Not at all,' replied the merchant; the Buddha and his monks were coming to dinner.

Anāthapindika could hardly believe his ears. 'Did you say "the Buddha"?' he asked incredulously; had an enlightened Buddha truly come into the world? Could he go to visit him at once? 'This is not the time,' the merchant said testily, hurrying off again. 'You can go to talk to him early tomorrow morning.' Anāthapindika was so excited that he could scarcely sleep, and at dawn he hurried to the Bamboo Grove. As soon as he left the city, however, he was overcome with the dread that was so widespread in the Axial countries. He felt vulnerable. 'Light drained from the world, and he could see only darkness ahead.' Fearfully he pressed on, until he saw the Buddha pacing up and down in the morning light. When the Buddha saw Anāthapindika, he led him to a seat and called him by name. Like Yasa before him, the merchant was immediately cheered, and as he listened to the Buddha he felt the teaching rising from within with such authority that it seemed inscribed in his deepest soul. 'Superb, Lord!' he cried, and begged the Buddha to accept him as a lay disciple. The next day, he entertained the Buddha at his brother-in-law's house and invited him to visit his own city of Sāvatthī, the capital of the kingdom of Kosala.[19]

Sāvatthī was probably the most advanced of all the cities in the Ganges basin in the late sixth century. It was built on the south bank of the Rivati river, at the junction of two trade routes, and was inhabited by some 70,000 families. A leading center of commerce, it was home to many wealthy businessmen like Anāthapindika, and the city's name was said to derive from the word *sārvamatthī*, since it was a place where 'everything was attainable.' Sāvatthī was protected by imposing walls and watchtowers forty to fifty feet high; the main roads entered the city from the south and converged in a large open square in the town center.[20] Yet despite Sāvatthī's prosperity, Anāthapindika's feverish excitement at the prospect of meeting a real Buddha shows that many people felt a nagging void opening up in their lives. It was exactly the place for the Sangha.

Anāthapindika spared no expense in setting up a base for the Buddha. He searched hard for a suitable place, and eventually decided on a park owned by Prince Jeta, heir apparent to the throne of Kosala. The prince was reluctant to sell – until Anāthapindika brought cartloads of gold coins, which he spread all over the parkland until the ground was entirely covered with the money that he was prepared to offer. Only a small space near the gate remained, and Prince Jeta, realizing belatedly that this was no ordinary purchase and that it might be advisable to make a contribution, threw it in for free, building a gate-house on the spot. Then Anāthapindika made Jeta's Grove ready for the Sangha. He had 'open terraces laid out, gates constructed, audience halls erected, fire rooms, storehouses and cupboards built, walks leveled, wells prepared, baths and bathrooms installed, ponds excavated and pavilions made.'[21] This would become one of the most important centers of the Sangha.

Yet these were very elaborate arrangements for men who had embraced 'homelessness.' Within a short space of time, the Buddha had acquired three large parks, at Rājagaha, Kapilavatthu and Sāvatthī, where the monks could live and meditate, surrounded by lotos pools, lush mango trees and shady cloisters of palms. Other donors quickly followed Anāthapindika's example. As soon as they heard that the Buddha was teaching in Sāvatthī, three bankers from Kosambī on the Jumna river came to hear him preach in Jeta's Grove and promptly invited him to their own city. Each equipped a 'pleasure-park' (*ārāma*) for the Sangha there. They not only raised buildings at their own expense, but, like the other donors, they maintained the *ārāma*, providing for its upkeep themselves. King Bimbisāra employed so many servants for the Bamboo Grove that they filled an entire village. But the monks were not living in luxury. Though ample, the accommodation was simple and the huts sparsely furnished, as befitted followers of the Middle Way. Each *bhikkhu* had his own cell, but this was often just a partitioned-off area containing only a board to sleep on and a seat with jointed legs.[22]

The *bhikkhus* did not live in these *ārāmas* year-round, but still spent most of their time on the road. At first, most even traveled during the monsoon, but found that this gave offense. Other sects, such as the Jains, refused to travel during the rains, because they would do too much damage to the wildlife, and this violated the principle of *ahiṃsā.* Why did these followers of Sakyamūni continue their journeys during the monsoon, people began to ask, 'trampling down the new grass, distressing plants, and hurting many little creatures?'

Even the vultures, they pointed out, stayed in the treetops during this season. Why did the Buddha's monks alone feel obliged to trudge around the muddy paths and roads, taking no heed of anybody but themselves?[23]

The Buddha was sensitive to this kind of criticism, and when he heard about these complaints, he made the monsoon retreat (*vassa*) obligatory for all Sangha members. But he went one step further than the other wanderers, and invented the monastic communal life. Monks in the other sects either lived alone during the *vassa*, or they put up wherever they happened to be, sharing a forest clearing with ascetics who followed quite different *dhammas*. The Buddha ordered his *bhikkhus* to live together during the *vassa*, not with members of other sects; they could choose one of the *ārāmas* or a country settlement (*āvāsa*), which the monks built each year from scratch. Each *ārāma* and *āvāsa* had fixed boundaries; no monk was allowed to leave the retreat for more than a week during the three months of the monsoon, except for a very good reason. Gradually, the monks began to evolve a community life. They devised simple ceremonies, which took place in the assembly hall of their settlement. In the morning, they would meditate and listen to the instructions given by the Buddha or one of the senior monks. Then they set off with their bowls to the town to seek the day's provisions, and ate their main meal. In the afternoon there would be a siesta, followed by more meditation in the evening.

But above all, the *bhikkhus* had to learn to live together amicably. The inevitable difficulties of living with people whom they might not find personally congenial would put the equanimity they were supposed to have acquired in meditation to the test. It was no good radiating compassion to the four quarters of the earth if *bhikkhus* could not be kind to one another. There were times when the Buddha had to take his monks to task. Once he rebuked them for failing to take care of a *bhikkhu* who had dysentery.[24] On another occasion, when the Buddha and his entourage were traveling to Sāvatthī, a clique of monks went ahead to one of their local settlements and secured all the beds. Poor Sāriputta, who seems to have had a bad cough, had to spend the night outside under a tree. Such rudeness, the Buddha told the guilty monks, undermined the whole mission of the Sangha, since it would put people off the Dhamma.[25] But gradually, the best of the *bhikkhus* learned to set aside their own selfish inclinations and consider their fellows. The person who returned first from town with the almsfood made the hut ready for the others, setting out the seats and preparing the water for cooking. The one who arrived home last ate the leftovers and put everything away. 'We are very different in body, Lord,' one of the monks told the Buddha about his community, 'but we have, I think, only one mind.' Why should he not ignore his own likes and dislikes, and do only what the others wished? This *bhikkhu* felt lucky to be living the holy life with such companions.[26] In the communal life of the *vassa*, the Buddha had found another way to teach his monks to live for others.

King Pasenedi of Kosala was very impressed by the friendliness and cheerfulness of life in the Buddhist *ārāmas*. It was in marked contrast to that of the court, he told the Buddha, where selfishness, greed and aggression were the order of the day. Kings quarreled with other kings, *brahmins* with other *brahmins;* families and friends were constantly at loggerheads. But in the *ārāma*, he saw *bhikkhus* 'living together as uncontentiously as milk with water and looking at one another with kind eyes.' In other sects, he noticed that the ascetics looked so skinny and miserable that he could only conclude that their lifestyle did not agree with them. 'But here I see *bhikkhus* smiling and courteous, sincerely happy…alert, calm and unflustered, living on alms, their minds remaining as gentle as wild deer.' When he sat in council, the king remarked wryly, he was constantly interrupted and even heckled. But when the Buddha addressed a huge crowd of monks, none of them even coughed or cleared his throat.[27] The Buddha was creating an alternative way of life that brought the shortcomings of the new towns and states into sharp focus.

Some scholars believe that the Buddha saw such rulers as Pasenedi and Bimbisāra as partners in a program of political and social reform. They suggest that the Sangha was designed to counter the rampant individualism that was inevitable as society progressed from a tribal, communal ethos to a competitive, cutthroat market economy. The Sangha would be a blueprint for a different type of social organization, and its ideas would gradually filter down to the people. They point to the frequent juxtaposition of the Buddha and the *cakkavatti* in the texts: the Buddha was to reform human consciousness, they suggest, while the kings introduced social reforms.[28] More recently, however, other scholars have argued that far from endorsing monarchy and working with it in this way, the Buddha seemed highly critical of kingship and preferred the republican style of government that still prevailed in his native Sakka.[29]

It seems unlikely that the Buddha had such political ambitions; he would surely have regarded any involvement with a social program as an unhelpful 'clinging' to the profane world. But the Buddha was certainly trying to forge a new way of being human. The evident contentment of his *bhikkhus* showed that the experiment was working. The monks had not been infused by supernatural grace or reformed at the behest of a god. The method devised by the Buddha was a purely human initiative. His monks were learning to work on their natural powers as skillfully as a goldsmith might fashion a piece of dull metal and make it shining and beautiful, helping it to become more fully itself and achieve its potential. It seemed that it was possible to train people to live without selfishness and to be happy. If the *bhikkhus* had been gloomy or frustrated, this would probably show that their lifestyle was doing violence to their humanity. 'Unskillful' states, such as anger, guilt, unkindness, envy and greed, were avoided not because they had been forbidden by a god or were 'sinful' but because the indulgence of such emotions was found to be damaging to human nature. The compassion, courtesy, consideration, friendliness and kindness required by the monastic life constituted the new asceticism. But unlike the old, extreme *tapas,* it created harmony and balance. If cultivated assiduously, it could evoke the *ceto-vimutti* of Nibbāṇa, another eminently natural psychological state.

But the full Dhamma was only possible for monks. The noise and bustle of the ordinary Indian household would make meditation and yoga impossibilities, so only a monk who had left this world could achieve Nibbāṇa. A layman such as Anāthapindika, who engaged in commercial and reproductive activities that were fueled by desire, could not hope to extinguish the three fires of greed, hatred and delusion. The best that a lay disciple could achieve was rebirth next time in circumstances that were more favorable to enlightenment. The Noble Truths were not for laymen; they had to be 'realized' and this 'direct' knowledge could not be achieved without yoga, which was essential to the full Buddhist regimen.[30] Without the discipline of mindfulness, a doctrine such as *anattā* would make no sense. But the Buddha did not ignore the lay folk. It seems that there were two main lines of preaching: one for monks and another for the laity.

This becomes evident in the poignant story of Anāthapindika's death. When he became mortally ill, Sāriputta and Ānanda went to visit him, and Sāriputta preached a short sermon on the value of detachment: Anāthapindika should train himself not to cling to the senses, since this contact with the external world would trap him in *saṃsāra*. This, one might think, was basic Buddhist teaching, but Anāthapindika had never heard it before. As he listened, tears ran down his face. 'What is the matter, householder?' Ānanda asked anxiously. 'Are you feeling worse?' No, Anāthapindika protested; that was not the problem. It grieved him that 'even though I have waited on the Master and the contemplative *bhikkhus* for so many years, I have never heard talk on the Dhamma like that before.' This teaching was not given to the lay people, Sāriputta explained. It was only for those who had left the household life behind. That was not right, Anāthapindika replied. Householders should be instructed in such matters: there were some with only a little desire in them, who were ripe for enlightenment and could, therefore, achieve Nibbāṇa.[31]

Anāthapindika died that night and, we are told, was reborn in heaven as a 'stream-enterer' with only seven more lives ahead of him. This was doubtless seen as a blessing, but it seems a poor reward for his generosity and devoted service. To keep such essential teaching from lay folk seems unfair, but the idea that everybody should be on the same spiritual footing is essentially modern. Premodern religion was nearly always conducted on two tiers, with an elite who spent their whole lives studying and meditating on scripture, and gave instruction to the inevitably more ignorant laity. Full religious equality only becomes a possibility when everybody is literate and has access to the scriptures. The Buddhist canon was not written down until the first century B.C.E., and even then manuscripts were rare. Anybody who wanted to hear the Dhamma would have to go to the Buddha or to one of the monks.

What did the Sangha preach to the laity? Lay people had 'taken refuge' with the Buddha from the very first. Lay men and women would feed the monks and support them, acquiring merit that would get them good rebirths. The monks would also teach the laity how to live morally and perform good, purifying *kamma* that would advance their spiritual prospects. Everybody regarded this as a fair exchange. Some lay people, such as Anāthapindika, would spend a lot of time with the Buddha and the *bhikkhus.* They were encouraged to take five moral vows – a Dhamma for beginners. They must not take life; they must not steal, lie or take intoxicants; they must avoid sexual promiscuity. These were much the same as the practices required of Jain lay disciples. On the quarter (*uposatha*) days of each month, the Buddhist laity had special disciplines to replace the fasting and abstinence of the old Vedic *upavasatha,* which, in practice, made them live like novices to the Sangha for twenty-four hours: they abstained from sex, did not watch entertainments, dressed soberly, and ate no solid food until midday.[32] This gave them a taste of a fuller Buddhist life and might have inspired some to become monks.

Like any yogin, before the Buddhist monk could even begin to meditate, he had to undergo a moral training in compassion, self-control and mindfulness. The laity were never able to graduate to serious yoga, so they concentrated on this morality (*sila*), which the Buddha adapted to their station of life. Laymen and -women were thus building the foundation for a fuller spirituality, which would stand them in good stead in their next existence. Where monks learned 'skillful' techniques in meditation, the lay person focused on 'skillful' morality.[33] Giving alms to a *bhikkhu,* telling the truth at all times and behaving kindly and justly toward others helped them to develop a more wholesome state of mind, and to mitigate, if not wholly stamp out, the fires of egotism. This morality also had a practical advantage: it could encourage others to behave toward them in a similar manner. As a result, besides accruing merit in their next lives, they were learning ways of being happier in this one.

The Dhamma was very appealing to merchants and bankers like Anāthapindika who had no place in the Vedic system. The businessmen could appreciate the Buddha's 'skillful' ethics, because it was based on the principle of shrewd investment. It would yield a profitable return, in this existence and the next. Monks were trained to be mindful of their fleeting mental states; lay followers were directed to *appanada* (attentiveness) in their financial and social dealings.[34] The Buddha told them to save for an emergency, look after their dependents, give alms to *bhikkhus,* avoid debt, make sure that they had enough money for the immediate needs of their families, and invest money carefully.[35] They were to be thrifty, sensible and sober. In the *Sigālavada Sutta,* the most developed sermon on lay morality, Sigāla was instructed to avoid alcohol, late nights, gambling, laziness and bad company.[36] There is a lay version of the Fire Sermon, in which the disciple is urged to tend the three 'good fires': taking care of his dependents; caring for his wife, children and servants; and supporting the *bhikkhus* in all the different *sanghas.*[37]

But, as always, the cardinal virtue was compassion. One day King Pasenedi and his wife had a discussion in which each admitted that nothing was dearer to them than their own selves. This was obviously not a view that the Buddha could share, but when the king told him about this conversation, the Buddha did not chide him, launch into a discussion of *anattā,* or preach a sermon on the Eightfold Path. Instead, as usual, he entered into Pasenedi's viewpoint, and built on what was in his mind – not on what the Buddha thought should be there. He did not, therefore, tell the king that the self was a delusion, because without a life of regular yoga, he would not be able to 'see' this. Instead, he told him to consider this: if he found that there was nothing dearer to him than himself, it must also be true that other people also cherished their 'separate selves.' Therefore, the Buddha concluded, 'a person who loves the self, should not harm the self of others.'[38] He should follow what other traditions have called the Golden Rule: 'Do not do unto others as you would not have done unto you.'[39] Laymen could not extinguish their egotism entirely, but they could use their experience of selfishness to empathize with other people's vulnerability. This would take them beyond the excesses of ego and introduce them to *ahiṃsā.*

We see the way the Buddha preached to lay people in his famous sermon to the Kālāmans,[40] a people who lived on the northernmost fringe of the Ganges basin and who had once run a tribal republic, but were now subject to Kosala. Gradually, they were being drawn into the new urban civilization and were finding the experience unsettling and undermining. When the Buddha passed through their town of Kesaputta, they sent a delegation to ask his advice. One ascetic, one teacher after another had descended upon them, they explained; but each monk and *brahmin* expounded his own doctrines and reviled everybody else's. Not only did these *dhammas* contradict one another, they were also alien, coming as they did from the sophisticated mainstream culture. 'Which of these teachers was right and which wrong?' they asked. The Buddha replied that he could see why the Kālāmans were so confused. As always, he entered completely into their position. He did not add to their confusion by reeling off his own Dhamma, and giving them one more doctrine to contend with, but held an impromptu tutorial (reminiscent of the question-and-answer techniques of such other Axial sages as Socrates and Confucius) to help the Kālāmans work things out for themselves. He started by telling them that one of the reasons for their bewilderment was that they were expecting other people to tell them the answer, but when they looked into their own hearts, they would find that in fact they knew what was right already.

'Come, Kālāmans,' he said, 'do not be satisfied with hearsay or taking truth on trust.' People must make up their own minds on questions of morality. Was greed, for example, good or bad? 'Bad, Lord,' the Kālāmans replied. Had they noticed that when somebody is consumed by desire and determined to get what he wants, that he is likely to kill, steal or lie? Yes, the Kālāmans had observed this. And did not this type of behavior make the selfish person unpopular and, therefore, unhappy? And what about hatred, or clinging to what were obviously delusions instead of trying to see things as they really were? Did not these emotions all lead to pain and suffering? Step by step, he asked the Kālāmans to draw upon their own experience and perceive the effect of the 'three fires' of greed, hatred and ignorance. By the end of their discussion, the Kālāmans found that in fact they had known the Buddha's Dhamma already. 'That is why I told you not to rely on any teacher,' the Buddha concluded. 'When you know in yourselves that these things are "helpful" (*kusala*) and those "unhelpful" (*akusala*), then you should practice this ethic and stick to it, whatever anybody else tells you.'[41]

He had also convinced the Kālāmans that while they should avoid greed, hatred and delusion, it would also obviously be beneficial to practice the opposite virtues: 'non-greed, non-hatred and non-delusion.' If they cultivated benevolence, kindness and generosity, and tried to acquire a sound understanding of life, they would find that they were happier people. If there was another life to come (the Buddha did not impose the doctrine of reincarnation upon the Kālāmans, who might not have been familiar with it), then this good *kamma* might get them reborn as gods in heaven next time. If there was no other world, then this considerate and genial lifestyle might encourage others to behave in like manner toward themselves. At the very least, they would know that they had behaved well – and that was always a comfort. To help the Kālāmans build up this 'skillful' mentality, the Buddha taught them a meditative technique that was a lay person's version of the 'immeasurables.' First they must try to rid their minds of envy, feelings of ill will and delusion. Then they should direct feelings of loving-kindness in every direction. As they did so, they would experience an enhanced, enlarged existence. They would find that they were imbued with 'abundant, exalted, measureless loving-kindness'; they would break out of the confines of their own limited viewpoint and embrace the whole world. They would transcend the pettiness of egotism and, for a moment, experience an ecstasy that took them out of themselves, 'above, below, around and everywhere,' and would feel their hearts expand with disinterested equanimity.[42] Laymen and -women might not be able to attain the permanence of Nibbāṇa, but they could have intimations of that final release.

The Buddha was, therefore, teaching monks and lay folk alike a compassionate offensive to mitigate the egotism that prevailed in the aggressive new society and that debarred human beings from the sacred dimension of life. The skillful state that he was trying to promote is well expressed in this poem in the Pāli Canon:

> Let all beings be happy! Weak or strong, of high, middle or low estate,
> small or great, visible or invisible, near or far away,
> alive or still to be born – may they all be entirely happy!
>
> Let nobody lie to anybody or despise any single being anywhere.
> May nobody wish harm to any single creature, out of anger or hatred!
>
> Let us cherish all creatures, as a mother her only child!
> May our loving thoughts fill the whole world, above, below,
> across – without limit; a boundless goodwill toward the whole world,
> unrestricted, free of hatred and enmity![43]

A lay person who achieved this attitude would have advanced a long way along the spiritual path.

The scriptures do give us a few examples of lay disciples who practiced meditation outside the Sangha and reached Nibbāṇa, but these solitary *virtuosi* were the exception rather than the rule. It was thought that an Arahant could not continue to live the life of a householder: after achieving enlightenment, he would either join the Sangha immediately or he would die. This, apparently, is what happened to Suddhodana, the Buddha's father, who attained Nibbāṇa in the fifth year of his son's teaching mission and died the next day. When the Buddha heard the news, he returned to Kapilavatthu and stayed for a while in Nigrodha Park. This event led to a new development in the Sangha, which, it seems, the Buddha did not initially welcome.

While he was living in the Nigrodha *ārāma,* the Buddha was visited by his father's widow, Pajāpatī Gotamī: she was also the Buddha's aunt, and had become his foster-mother after the death of his own mother. Since she was now free, she told her nephew, she wanted to be ordained in the Sangha. The Buddha adamantly refused. There was no question of admitting women to the Order. He would not change his mind, even though Pajāpatī begged him three times to reconsider and she left his presence very sadly. A few days later, the Buddha set out for Vesālī, the capital of the republic of Videha on the northern bank of the Ganges. He often stayed in the *ārāma* there, which had a hall with a high-gabled roof. One morning, Ānanda was horrified to find Pajāpatī sobbing on the porch with a crowd of other Sakyan women. She had cut off her hair, put on the yellow robe and had walked all the way from Kapilavatthu. Her feet were swollen, and she was filthy and exhausted. 'Gotamī,' cried Ānanda; 'What are you doing here in such a state? And why are you crying?' 'Because the Blessed One will not have women in the Sangha,' Pajāpatī replied. Ānanda was concerned. 'Wait here,' he said, 'I will ask the Tathāgata about this.'

But the Buddha still refused to consider the matter. This was a serious moment. If he continued to bar women from the Sangha, it meant that he considered that half of the human race was ineligible for enlightenment. But the

Dhamma was supposed to be for everybody: for gods, animals, robbers, men of all castes – were women alone to be excluded? Was rebirth as a man the best they could hope for? Ānanda tried another tack. 'Lord,' he asked, 'are women capable of becoming "stream-enterers" and, eventually, Arahants?' 'They are, Ānanda,' the Buddha replied. 'Then surely it would be a good thing to ordain Pajāpatī,' Ānanda pleaded, and reminded his master of her kindness to him after his mother had died. The Buddha reluctantly conceded defeat. Pajāpatī could enter the Sangha if she accepted eight strict rules. These provisions made it clear that the nuns (*bhikkhunīs*) were an inferior breed. A nun must always stand when in the presence of a male *bhikkhu*, even one who was young or newly ordained; nuns must always spend the *vassa* retreat in an *ārāma* with male monks, not by themselves; they must receive instruction from a *bhikkhu* once every fortnight; they could not hold their own ceremonies; a nun who had committed a grave offense must do penance before the monks as well as the *bhikkhunīs;* a nun must request ordination from both the male and the female Sangha; she must never rebuke a *bhikkhu,* though any monk could rebuke her; nor could she preach to *bhikkhus.* Pajāpatī gladly accepted these regulations and was duly ordained, but the Buddha was still uneasy. If women had not been admitted, he told Ānanda, the Dhamma would have been practiced for a thousand years; now it would last a mere five hundred years. A tribe with too many women would become vulnerable and be destroyed; similarly, no Sangha with women members could last long. They would fall upon the Order like mildew on a field of rice.[44]

What are we to make of this misogyny? The Buddha had always preached to women as well as to men. Once he had given permission, thousands of women became *bhikkhunīs*, and the Buddha praised their spiritual attainments, said that they could become the equals of the monks, and prophesied that he would not die until he had enough wise monks *and* nuns, lay men *and* lay women followers.[45] There seems to be a discrepancy in the texts, and this has led some scholars to conclude that the story of his grudging acceptance of women and the eight regulations was added later and reflects a chauvinism in the Order. By the first century B.C.E., some of the monks certainly blamed women for their own sexual desires, which were impeding them from enlightenment, and regarded women as universal obstacles to spiritual advance. Other scholars argue that the Buddha, enlightened as he was, could not escape the social conditioning of the time, and that he could not imagine a society that was not patriarchal. They point out that, despite the Buddha's initial reluctance, the ordination of women was a radical act that, perhaps for the first time, gave women an alternative to domesticity.[46]

While this is true, there is a difficulty for women that should not be glossed over. In the Buddha's mind, women may well have been inseparable from the 'lust' that made enlightenment an impossibility. It did not occur to him to take his wife with him, as some of the renouncers did, when he left home to begin his quest. He simply assumed that she could not be the partner in his liberation. But this was not because he found sexuality disgusting, like the Christian Fathers of the Church, but because he was attached to his wife. The scriptures contain a passage which, scholars agree, is almost certainly a monkish interpolation. 'Lord, how are we to treat women?' Ānanda asked the Buddha in the last days of his life. 'Do not look at them, Ānanda.' 'If we do not see them, how should we treat them?' 'Do not speak to them, Ānanda.'

'And if we have to speak to them?' 'Mindfulness must be observed, Ānanda.'[47] The Buddha may not have personally subscribed to this full-blown misogyny, but it is possible that these words reflect a residual unease that he could not overcome.

If the Buddha did harbor negative feelings about women, this was typical of the Axial Age. Sad to say, civilization has not been kind to women. Archeological discoveries indicate that women were sometimes highly esteemed in pre-urban societies, but the rise of the military states and the specialization of the early cities led to a decline in their position. They became the property of men, were excluded from most professions, and were subjected to the sometimes draconian control of their husbands in some of the ancient law codes. Elite women managed to hold on to some shreds of power, but in the Axial countries women suffered a further loss of status at about the time that the Buddha was preaching in India. In Iran, Iraq, and, later, in the Hellenistic states, women were veiled and confined in harems, and misogynistic ideas flourished. The women of classical Athens (500–323) were particularly disadvantaged and almost entirely secluded from society; their chief virtues were said to be silence and submission. The early Hebrew traditions had exalted the exploits of such women as Miriam, Deborah and Jael, but after the prophetic reform of the faith, women were relegated to second-class status in Jewish law. It is notable that in a country such as Egypt, which did not participate initially in the Axial Age, there was a more liberal attitude to women.[48] It seems that the new spirituality contained an inherent hostility toward the female that has lasted until our own day. The Buddha's quest was masculine in its heroism: the determined casting off of all restraints, the rejection of the domestic world and women, the solitary struggle, and the penetration of new realms are attitudes that have become emblematic of male virtue. It is only in the modern world that this attitude has been challenged. Women have sought their own 'liberation' (they have even used the same word as the Buddha); they too have rejected the old authorities, and set off on their own lonely journey.

The Buddha predicted that women would blight the Order, but in fact the first major crisis in the Sangha was caused by a clash of male egos.[49] According to Buddhist principles, a fault is not culpable unless the perpetrator realizes that he has done wrong. In Kosambī, a sincere and learned monk was suspended, but protested that his punishment was unfair, since he had not realized that he was committing an offense. The Kosambī *bhikkhus* at once divided into hostile factions and the Buddha was so distressed by the schism that at one point he went off to live by himself in the forest, forming a friendship with an elephant who had also suffered from aggressive peers. Hatred, the Buddha said, was never appeased by more hatred; it could only be defused by friendship and sympathy.[50] He could see that both camps had right on their side, but the egotism of all the *bhikkhus* involved made it impossible for them to see the other point of view, even though the Buddha tried to make each faction understand the position of the other. He told Sāriputta and Pajāpatī, now head of the women's Sangha, to treat both sides with respect; Anāthapindika was instructed to give donations impartially to both camps. But the Buddha did not impose a solution: the answer must come from the participants themselves. Eventually, the suspended *bhikkhu* climbed down: even though he had not known it at the time, he *had* committed a fault. Immediately, he was reinstated and the quarrel came to an end.[51]

The story tells us a good deal about the early Sangha. There was no tight organization and no central authority. It was closer to the *sanghas* of the old republics, where all the members of the council were equal, than to the new monarchies. The Buddha refused to be an authoritative and controlling ruler, and did not resemble the Father Superior of later Christian religious orders. Indeed, it was probably inaccurate to speak of *an* Order; there were rather a number of different orders, each of them situated in a particular region of the Ganges basin. Nevertheless, the members all shared the same Dhamma and followed the same lifestyle. Every six years, the scattered *bhikkhus* and *bhikkhunīs* would come together to recite a common confession of faith, called the Pāṭimokkha ('bond').[52] As its name implies, its purpose was to bind the Sangha together:

> Refraining from all that is harmful,
> Attaining what is skillful,
> And purifying one's own mind;
> This is what the Buddhas teach.
>
> Forbearance and patience are the highest of all austerities;
> And the Buddhas declare that Nibbāṇa is the supreme value.
> Nobody who hurts another has truly 'Gone Forth' from the home life.
> Nobody who injures others is a true monk.
>
> No faultfinding, no harming, restraint,
> Knowing the rules regarding food, the single bed and chair,
> Application in the higher perception derived from meditation –
> This is what the Awakened Ones teach.[53]

The Buddha attached great importance to this ceremony, which corresponded to the plenary assemblies that had characterized the republics. Nobody was allowed to miss the Pāṭimokkha, since it was the only thing that held the early Sangha together.

Much later, after the Buddha's death, this simple recitation was replaced by a more elaborate and complex assembly, held by each local community in each region once a fortnight, on the *uposatha* days. This change marked the transition of the Sangha from a sect to an Order. Instead of chanting the Dhamma, which distinguished them from the other sects, the monks and nuns now recited the rules of the Sangha and confessed their transgressions to one another. By this time, the Sangha's regulations were more numerous than they had been in the Buddha's day. Some scholars argue that it took two or three centuries for the Rule, as recorded in the Vinaya, to take its final form, but some believe that, at least substantially, the spirit of the Order can be traced back to the Buddha himself.[54]

The Sangha is the heart of Buddhism, because its lifestyle embodies externally the inner state of Nibbāṇa.[55] Monks and nuns must 'Go Forth,' not only from the household life but even from their own selves. A *bhikkhu* and *bhikkhunī,* almsman and almswoman, have renounced the 'craving' that goes with getting and spending, depend entirely on what they are given and learn to be happy with the bare minimum. The lifestyle of the Sangha enables its members to meditate, and thus to dispel the fires of ignorance, greed and hatred that bind us to the wheel of suffering. The ideal of compassion and communal love teaches them to lay aside their own egotism and live for others. By making these attitudes habitual, nuns and monks can acquire that unshakable inner peace which is Nibbāṇa, the goal of the holy life. The Sangha is one of the oldest surviving voluntary institutions on earth; only the Jain order can boast a similar antiquity. Its endurance tells us something important about humanity and human life. The great empires, manned by vast armies of soldiers, have all crumbled, but the community of *bhikkhus* has lasted some 2,500 years. It is a polarity adumbrated in the early Buddhist legends that juxtapose the Buddha with the *cakkavatti.* The message seems to be that it is not by protecting and defending yourself that you survive, but by giving yourself away.

But even though the members of the Sangha had all turned their backs on the lifestyle of the vast majority of the population, the people at large did not resent them but found them profoundly attractive. The lay folk did not see the *bhikkhus* and *bhikkhunīs* as grim renouncers, but sought them out. This again tells us that the lifestyle devised by the Buddha was felt not to be inhuman but to be deeply humane. The *ārāmas* were not lonely outposts; kings, *brahmins*, merchants, businessmen, courtesans, aristocrats, and members of the other sects flocked to them. Pasenedi and Bimbisāra constantly dropped in to ask the Buddha's advice, while he was sitting in the evening beside a lotos pool, or reclining in the porch of his hut, watching the moths fly into the candle flame. We read of crowds of ascetics pouring into the Buddhist settlements; delegations would come to ask the Buddha a question; noblemen and merchants would arrive, mounted on elephants, and the gilded youth of a district would ride out en masse to invite the Buddha to dinner.

In the midst of all this excitement and activity was the quiet, controlled figure of the Buddha, the new, 'awakened' man. He remains opaque and unknowable to those of us who are incapable of his complete self-abandonment, because after his enlightenment he became impersonal, though never unkind or cold. There is no sign of struggle or effort on his part; as he exclaimed on the night of his enlightenment, he had completed everything that he had to do. He was the Tathāgata, the man who had disappeared. He had no personal attachments and had no aggressively doctrinaire opinions. In the Pāli texts he is often compared to nonhuman beings, not because he was considered unnatural, but because people did not know how to classify him.

One day, a *brahmin* found the Buddha sitting under a tree, composed and contemplative. 'His faculties were at rest, his mind was still, and everything about him breathed self-discipline and serenity.' The sight filled the *brahmin* with awe. The Buddha reminded him of a tusker elephant; there was the same impression of enormous strength and massive potential brought under control and channeled into a great peace. There were discipline, restraint and complete serenity. The *brahmin* had never seen a man like that before. 'Are you a god, sir?' he asked. 'No,' replied the Buddha. 'Are you becoming an angel...or a spirit?' persisted the *brahmin*. Again, the answer was 'No.' 'Are you a human being?' asked the *brahmin*, as a last resort, but again the Buddha replied that he was not. He had become something else. The world had not seen humanity like this since the last Buddha had lived on earth, thousands of years ago. Once he had been a god in a previous life, the Buddha explained; he had lived as an animal and as an ordinary man, but everything that had confined him to the old, unregenerate humanity had been extinguished, 'cut off at the root, chopped off like a palm stump, done away with.' Had the *brahmin* ever seen a red lotos that had begun its life underwater rising above the pond, until it no longer touched the surface? the Buddha asked. 'So I too was born and grew up in the world,' he told his visitor, 'but I have transcended the world and am no longer touched by it.' By attaining Nibbāṇa in this life, he had revealed a new potential in human nature. It was possible to live in this world of pain, at peace, in control and in harmony with oneself and the rest of creation. But to achieve this tranquil immunity, a man or woman had to break free of his or her egotism and live entirely for other beings. Such a death to self was not a darkness, however frightening it might seem to an outsider; it made people fully aware of their own nature, so that they lived at the peak of their capacity. How should the *brahmin* categorize the Buddha? 'Remember me,' the Buddha told him, 'as one who has woken up.'[56]

6 PARINIBBĀNA

ONE AFTERNOON, FORTY-FIVE years after the Buddha's enlightenment, King Pasenedi called on him unexpectedly in the town of Medaḷumpa in Sakka. He was now an old man, and had remarked recently to the Buddha that political life was becoming more and more violent. Kings were 'drunk with authority,' 'obsessed with greed,' and constantly engaged in 'fighting battles using elephants, horses, chariots and infantry.'[1] The Ganges basin seemed ablaze with destructive egotism. For years, Kosala had been fending off the Magadhan army, which was making a bid to achieve sole hegemony in the region. And Pasenedi himself was desolate. His beloved wife had died recently, and he had fallen into a profound depression. This was what happened when you put your trust in other moribund human beings. Pasenedi no longer felt at home anywhere in the world; in a parody of the wandering monk's 'Going Forth,' he had taken to leaving his palace and driving for miles with his army, going aimlessly from one place to another. He had been out on one of these pointless excursions into Sakka when he heard that the Buddha was staying in the vicinity. Immediately he felt a great longing to be in his presence. The Buddha, he reflected, reminded him of a huge tree: he was quiet, aloof, above the petty disturbances of the world, but you could shelter there in a crisis. Immediately, he drove to Medaḷumpa, and when the road became impassable, he dismounted, left his sword and royal turban with his general, Dīgha Kārāyana, and made his way to the Buddha's hut on foot. When the Buddha opened the door, Pasenedi kissed his feet. 'Why are you doing this poor old body such honor?' asked the Buddha. Because the *ārāma* was such a comfort to him, replied the king; because the peace of the Sangha was so different from the selfishness, violence and greed of his court. But above all, Pasenedi concluded: 'The Blessed One is eighty and I am eighty.'[2] They were two old men together, and they should express their affection for each other in this dark world.

When Pasenedi left the hut and returned to the place where he had left Dīgha Kārāyana, he found that the general had gone and had taken the royal insignia with him. He hurried to the place where the army had encamped and found the spot deserted; only one of the ladies-in-waiting remained behind, with one horse and a single sword. Dīgha Kārāyana had gone back to Sāvatthī, she told the king, and was organizing a coup to put Prince Viḍuḍabha, Pasenedi's heir, on the throne. Pasenedi should not return to Sāvatthī if he valued his life. The old king decided to go to Magadha, since he was related to its royal house by marriage. But it was a long journey, and on the way, Pasenedi had to eat coarser food than usual and drink fetid water. When he arrived in Rājagaha the gates had closed, and Pasenedi was forced to sleep in a cheap lodging house. That night, he became violently ill with dysentery and died before dawn. The serving lady, who had done her best for the old man, began to rouse the whole city: 'My lord the king of Kosala, who ruled two countries, has died a pauper's death and is now lying in a common pauper's rest home outside a foreign city!'[3]

The Buddha had always seen old age as a symbol of the *dukkha* which afflicted all mortal beings. As Pasenedi had remarked, he himself was now old. Ānanda, who was far from young himself, had recently been dismayed by the change in his master. His skin was wrinkled, his limbs were flaccid, his body was bent and his senses seemed to be failing. 'So it is, so it is, Ānanda,' the Buddha agreed.[4] Old age was indeed cruel. But the story of the Buddha's last years dwells less on the aesthetic disaster of aging than on the vulnerability of the old. Ambitious young men rise up against their elders, sons kill their own fathers. In this final phase of the Buddha's life, the texts dwell on the terror of a world where all sense of sacredness is lost. Egotism reigns supreme; envy, hatred, greed and ambition are unmitigated by compassion and loving-kindness. People who stand in the way of a man's craving are ruthlessly eliminated. All decency and respect have disappeared. By stressing the dangers that the Buddha had tried to counter for nearly fifty years, the scriptures force us to confront the ruthlessness and violence of the society against which he had launched his campaign of selflessness and loving-kindness.

Not even the Sangha was immune from this profane spirit. Eight years earlier, the Order had once again been threatened by schism and had been implicated in a plot to kill King Bimbisāra, another old man, who had been the Buddha's devoted follower for thirty-seven years. We find a full account of this rebellion only in the Vinaya. It may not be entirely historical, but it issues a warning: even the principles of the Sangha could be subverted and made lethal. According to the Vinaya, the culprit was Devadatta, the Buddha's brother-in-law, who had entered the Sangha after the Buddha's first trip home to Kapilavatthu. The later commentaries tell us that Devadatta had been malicious from his youth, and had always been the sworn enemy of the young Gotama when the two were growing up together. The Pāli texts, however, know nothing of this and present Devadatta as an unexceptionally devout monk. He appears to have been a brilliant orator, and as the Buddha got older, Devadatta became resentful of his hold over the Order. He decided to build his own power base. Devadatta had lost all sense of the religious life, and began ruthlessly to promote himself. His horizons had narrowed: instead of reaching out expansively to the four corners of the earth in love, he was centered solely on his own career and consumed by hatred and envy. First he approached Prince Ajātasattu, son and heir of King Bimbisāra and commander-in-chief of the Magadhan army. He impressed the prince with flashy displays of *iddhi,* a sure sign that he was profaning his yogic powers. But the prince became Devadatta's patron: every day, he sent five hundred carriages to Devadatta in the *ārāma* of Vulture's Peak, just outside Rājagaha, together with unseemly mounds of food for the *bhikkhus.* Devadatta became a favored court monk; the flattery went to his head and he decided to seize control of the Sangha. But when the Buddha was warned of his brother-in-law's activities, he was not disturbed. Unskillful behavior on this scale could only bring Devadatta to an unsavory end.[5]

Devadatta made his first move while the Buddha was staying in the Bamboo Grove outside Rājagaha. In front of a huge assembly of *bhikkhus,* Devadatta formally asked the Buddha to resign and hand over the Sangha to him. 'The Blessed One is now old, aged, burdened with years... and has reached the last stage of his life,' he said unctuously. 'Let him now rest.' The

Buddha adamantly refused: he would not even hand the Sangha over to Sāriputta and Moggallāna, his two most eminent disciples. Why should he appoint such a lost soul as Devadatta to the position? Humiliated and furious, Devadatta left the *ārāma* vowing revenge. The Buddha was not much concerned about the leadership of the Order. He had always maintained that the Sangha did not need a central authority figure, since each monk was responsible for himself. But any attempt to sow dissension, as Devadatta had done, was anathema. An atmosphere of egotism, ambition, hostility and competitiveness was absolutely incompatible with the spiritual life and would negate the raison d'être of the Sangha. The Buddha, therefore, publicly dissociated himself and his Order from Devadatta and told Sāriputta to denounce him in Rājagaha. 'Formerly,' he explained, 'Devadatta had one nature; now he has another.' But the damage had been done. Some of the townsfolk believed that the Buddha was jealous of Devadatta's new popularity with the prince; the more judicious, however, reserved judgment.[6]

Meanwhile, Devadatta approached Prince Ajātasattu with a proposition. In the old days, he said, people lived longer than they did now. King Bimbisāra was lingering on, and perhaps Ajātasattu would never sit on the throne. Why did he not slay his father, while he, Devadatta, killed the Buddha? Why should these two old men stand in their way? Together, Devadatta and Ajātasattu would make a great team and achieve marvelous things. The prince liked the idea, but when he tried to slip into the king's inner sanctum with a dagger strapped to his thigh, he was arrested and confessed all. Some of the officers of the army wanted to put the whole Sangha to death when they heard of Devadatta's role in the assassination attempt, but Bimbisāra pointed out that the Buddha had already repudiated Devadatta and could not be held responsible for the deeds of this miscreant. When Ajātasattu was brought before him, the king asked him sadly why he had wanted to kill him. 'I want the kingdom, sire,' Ajātasattu replied with disarming frankness. Bimbisāra had not been the Buddha's disciple for so long for nothing. 'If you want the kingdom, Prince,' he said simply, 'it is yours.'[7] Like Pasenedi, he was probably aware of the unskillful and aggressive passions that were required in politics, and perhaps wanted to devote his last years to the spiritual life. His abdication did him no good, however. With the support of the army, Ajātasattu arrested his father and starved him to death.

The new king then backed Devadatta's scheme to kill the Buddha, providing him with trained assassins from the army. But as soon as the first of these approached the Buddha with a bow and arrow, he was overcome with terror and rooted to the spot. 'Come friend,' the Buddha said gently. 'Do not be afraid.' Because he had seen the error of his ways, his crime was forgiven. The Buddha then gave the soldier instruction appropriate for the layman and in a very short time the repentant killer had become a disciple. One by one, his fellow conspirators followed suit.[8] After this, Devadatta was forced to take the matter into his own hands. First he pushed a huge boulder over a cliff hoping to crush the Buddha, but succeeded only in grazing the Buddha's foot. Next he hired a famously ferocious elephant called Naligiri, which he let loose on the Buddha. But as soon as Naligiri saw his prey, he was overcome by the waves of love that emanated from the Buddha, lowered his trunk, and stood still while the Buddha stroked his forehead, explaining to him that violence would not help him in his next life. Naligiri took dust off the Buddha's feet with his trunk, sprinkled it over his own forehead, and retreated backward, gazing yearningly at the Buddha all the while until he was out of sight. Then he ambled peaceably back to the stables, a reformed beast from that day forth.[9]

Seeing that the Buddha seemed proof against these assaults, the conspirators changed their tactics. Ajātasattu, who had succeeded in his own bid for power, dropped Devadatta and became one of the Buddha's lay disciples. Devadatta was now on his own and tried to find support within the Sangha. He appealed to some of the younger and more inexperienced monks of Vesālī, arguing that the Buddha's Middle Way was an unacceptable deviation from tradition. Buddhists should return to the tougher ideals of the more traditional ascetics. Devadatta proposed five new rules: all members of the Sangha should live in the forests rather than in the *ārāmas* during the monsoon; they must rely solely on alms and must not accept invitations to eat at the houses of the laity; instead of new robes, they must wear only cast-off rags picked up from the streets; they must sleep in the open instead of in huts; and they must never eat the flesh of any living being.[10] These five rules may represent the historical kernel in the story of Devadatta's defection. Some of the more conservative *bhikkhus* may well have been concerned that standards were slipping and could have attempted to break away from the main Sangha. Devadatta might have been associated with this reform movement, and his enemies, the proponents of the Buddha's Middle Way, could have blackened Devadatta's name by inventing the dramatic legends that we find in the Vinaya.

When Devadatta published his five rules and asked the Buddha to make them obligatory for the whole Sangha, the Buddha refused, pointing out that any monk who wished to live in this way was perfectly free to do so, but that coercion in these matters was against the spirit of the Order. Monks must make up their own minds and not be forced to follow anybody else's directives. Devadatta was jubilant. The Buddha had refused his pious request! He announced triumphantly to his followers that the Buddha was given over to luxury and self-indulgence and that it was their duty to withdraw from their corrupt brethren.[11] With five hundred young monks, Devadatta decamped to Gayāsisa Hill outside Rājagaha, while the Buddha dispatched Sāriputta and Moggallāna to win the rebellious *bhikkhus* back. When Devadatta saw them approaching, he immediately assumed that they had deserted the Buddha and come to join him. Elated, he called an assembly and addressed his disciples far into the night. Then, pleading that his back was paining him, he retired to bed, handing the floor to Sāriputta and Moggallāna. Once these two loyal elders began to speak, they were soon able to persuade the *bhikkhus* to return to the Buddha, who received them back without reprisals.[12] Some texts tell us that Devadatta committed suicide; others that he died before he was able to be reconciled with the Buddha. Whatever the truth of these stories, they make a telling point about the suffering of old age; they also form a cautionary tale. Even the Sangha was not immune to the selfishness, ambition and dissension that was so rampant in public life.

The Buddha reflected on this danger in the last year of his life. He was now eighty years old. King Ajātasattu was by this time firmly established on the throne of Magadha and frequently visited the Buddha. He was planning an offensive against the republics of Malla, Videha, Licchavi, Koliya and Vajji, all to the east of his kingdom, who had formed a defensive confederacy known collectively as 'the Vajjians.' The king was determined to wipe them off the map and absorb them into his kingdom, but before he launched his attack, he sent his minister Vassakāra, a *brahmin*, to tell the Buddha what he was about to do and to listen carefully to his comments. The Buddha was cryptic. He told Vassakāra that as long as the Vajjians remained true to the republican traditions; held 'frequent and well-attended meetings'; lived together in concord; respected the older men, listening carefully to their advice; and observed the laws and pieties of their ancestors, King Ajātasattu would not be able to defeat them. Vassakāra listened attentively and told the Buddha that, since the Vajjians at present met all these conditions, they were in fact impregnable. He went back to break the news to the king.[13] Buddhist tradition, however, has it that shortly after this, King Ajātasattu did manage to defeat the Vajjians: he achieved this feat by sending spies into the republics to sow discord among the leaders. So there was a poignancy and urgency in the Buddha's next words, after the door had closed behind Vassakāra. He applied the same conditions to the Sangha: as long as its members respected the senior *bhikkhus*, held frequent assemblies, and remained absolutely true to the Dhamma, the Sangha would survive.

The tribal republics were doomed. They belonged to the past and would shortly be swept away by the new militant monarchies. King Pasenedi's son would soon defeat and massacre the Sakyans, the Buddha's own people. But the Buddha's Sangha was a new, up-to-date, and spiritually skillful version of the old republican governments. It would hold true to values that the more violent and coercive monarchies were in danger of forgetting. But this was a dangerous world. The Sangha could not survive the internal dissension, disrespect for elders, lack of loving-kindness, and superficiality that had surfaced during the Devadatta scandal. *Bhikkhus* and *bhikkhunīs* must be mindful, spiritually alert, energetic and faithful to the meditative disciplines that alone could bring them enlightenment. The Order would not decline as long as monks avoided such unskillful pursuits as 'gossiping, lazing around, and socializing; as long as they have no unprincipled friends and avoid falling under such people's spell; as long as they do not stop halfway in their quest and remain satisfied with a mediocre level of spirituality.'[14] If they failed in this, the Sangha would become indistinguishable from any secular institution; it would fall prey to the vices of the monarchies and become hopelessly corrupt.

After the meeting with Vassakāra, the Buddha decided to leave Rājagaha and travel north in order to spend the *vassa* retreat in Vesālī. It is as though the revelation of King Ajātasattu's plans to 'exterminate and destroy' the Vajjians had momentarily repelled him and made him aware of the affinity he felt for the beleaguered republics. He had spent most of his working life in Kosala and Maghada and had fulfilled an important mission there. But now, an old man who had himself suffered from the aggression that fueled the political life of these kingdoms, he headed out into the more marginal regions of the Ganges basin.

Slowly, with a large entourage of monks, the Buddha journeyed through Magadhan territory, first to Nālanda and then to Pāṭaligāma (the modern Patna), later the capital of the great Buddhist king Aṣoka (c. 269–232 B.C.E.), who would create a monarchy that eschewed violence and tried to embody the compassionate ethic of the Dhamma. The Buddha noticed the great fortresses that were being built by the Magadhan ministers in preparation for the coming war with the Vajjians, and prophesied the city's future greatness. There a delegation of lay disciples put a rest house at the Buddha's disposal, laying down carpets and hanging a great oil lamp, and the Buddha sat up all night preaching the version of the Dhamma that had been adapted to the needs of the laity. He pointed out that the prudence of skillful behavior could benefit a virtuous man or woman even in this world, and would ensure that in their next lives they would be farther along the route to enlightenment.[15]

Finally, the Buddha arrived at Vesālī. At first everything seemed as it had always been. He lodged in a mango grove belonging to Ambapālī, one of the town's leading courtesans. She came out to greet the Buddha with a fleet of state carriages, sat at his feet to listen to the Dhamma, and invited him to dine. Just as he had given his consent, the members of the Licchavi tribe who were living in Vesālī sallied forth in a body to invite the Buddha themselves, riding in a splendid procession of brilliantly colored carriages. It was a marvelous sight, and the Buddha smiled when he saw it, telling his *bhikkhus* that now they had some idea of the magnificence of the gods in heaven. The Licchavis sat around the Buddha, who 'spurred them on, inspired and encouraged' them with talk of the Dhamma. At the end of this discourse, the Licchavis issued their invitation to dinner, and when the Buddha told them that he was already engaged to eat with Ambapālī, they did not lose their good humor, but snapped their fingers, crying 'Oh the mango girl has beaten us, the mango girl has outwitted us!' That night, at dinner, the courtesan donated the mango grove to the Sangha, and the Buddha stayed for a while there, preaching to his *bhikkhus*. There was the usual bustle, glamour and excitement around the Buddha and, at its heart, the constant exhortation to an intense interior life of mindfulness and meditation.[16]

But then the picture began to darken. The Buddha left

Vesālī with his monks and took up residence in the nearby village of Beluvagāmaka. After they had stayed there a while, he suddenly dismissed his monks: they should go back to Vesālī and put up for the monsoon retreat wherever they could. He and Ānanda would stay on in Beluvagāmaka. A new solitude had entered the Buddha's life, and from this point he seemed to shun the larger cities and towns and to seek out ever more obscure locations. It was as though he were already beginning to leave the world. After the *bhikkhus* had left, the Buddha became seriously ill, but with great self-control he suppressed the pain and overcame his sickness. It was not right for him to die yet and attain the Ultimate Nibbāṇa *(parinibbāṇa)*, which would complete the enlightenment he had won under the bodhi tree. First he must bid the Sangha farewell. The Buddha, therefore, recovered, left his sickroom, and came out to sit with Ānanda on the porch of the hut in which he was staying.

His illness had shaken Ānanda to the core. 'I am used to seeing the Blessed One healthy and fit,' he told the Buddha tremulously as he sat down beside him. For the first time he had realized that his master could die. 'I felt my body go rigid,' he said, 'I could not see straight, my mind was confused.' But he had found comfort in one thought: the Buddha would not die until he had made some practical arrangements about the succession and the government of the Sangha, which would have to change once the master had departed. The Buddha sighed. 'What does the Sangha expect of me, Ānanda?' he asked patiently. The *bhikkhus* all knew everything he had to teach them. There was no secret doctrine for a few chosen leaders. Such thoughts as 'I must govern the Sangha' or 'The Sangha depends on me' did not occur to an enlightened man. 'I am an old man, Ānanda, eighty years old,' the Buddha went on inexorably. 'My body can only get about with the help of makeshifts, like an old cart.' The one activity that brought him ease and refreshment was meditation, which introduced him to the peace and release of Nibbāṇa. And so it must be for every single *bhikkhu* and *bhikkhunī*. 'Each of you must make himself his island, make himself and no one else his refuge.' No Buddhist could depend upon another person and need one of their number to lead the Order. 'The Dhamma – and the Dhamma alone – was his refuge.'[17] How could the *bhikkhus* become self-reliant? They knew the answer already: by meditation, concentration, mindfulness and a disciplined detachment from the world. The Sangha needed no one to govern it, no central authority. The whole point of the Buddhist lifestyle was to achieve an inner resource that made such dependence quite ludicrous.

But Ānanda had not yet achieved Nibbāṇa. He was not a skilled yogin and had not managed to achieve this degree of self-sufficiency. He was personally attached to his master and would become the model of those Buddhists who were not ready for such yogic heroism, but needed a more human devotion *(bhakhti)* to the Buddha to encourage them. Ānanda had another shock a few days later, when a novice brought them news of the deaths of Sāriputta and Moggallāna in Nālanda. Yet again, the Buddha was mildly exasperated to see Ānanda's distress. What did he expect? Was it not the essence of the Dhamma that nothing lasted forever and that there was always separation from everything and everybody that we love? Did Ānanda imagine that Sāriputta had taken with him the laws and insights by which Buddhists lived, or that the code of virtue and the knowledge of meditation had also departed from the Sangha? 'No, Lord,' protested the hapless Ānanda. It was just that he could not help remembering how generous Sāriputta had been to them all, how he had enriched and aided them by his tireless exposition of the Dhamma. It had been heartbreaking to see his begging bowl and robe, which the novice had brought to the Buddha when he came to break the news. 'Ānanda,' said the Buddha again, 'each of you should make himself his island, make himself and no one else his refuge; each of you must make the Dhamma his island, the Dhamma and nothing else his refuge.'[18]

Far from being distressed about the deaths of his two closest disciples, the Buddha was overjoyed that they had attained their *parinibbāṇa,* their ultimate release from the frailties of mortality. It was a joy to him to have had two such disciples, who were so beloved by the whole Sangha! How could he be sorrowful and lament, when they had reached the final goal of their quest?[19] Nevertheless, for the unenlightened, there is a poignancy and sadness in the Buddha's end. None of the inner circle was left except for Ānanda. The texts try to disguise it, but there were no more excited crowds and colorful dinners with friends. Instead, the Buddha and Ānanda, two old men, struggled on alone, experiencing the weariness of survival and the passing away of companions which constitutes the true tragedy of old age. That even the Buddha may have had some intimations of this and felt potentially bereft is suggested by the last appearance of Māra, his shadow-self, in his life. He and Ānanda had just spent the day alone together at one of the many shrines in Vesālī, and the Buddha remarked that it was possible for a fully enlightened man like himself to live out the rest of this period of history, if he wished. He was, the texts tell us, giving Ānanda a broad hint. If he begged him to stay in the world, out of compassion for the gods and men who needed his guidance, the Buddha had the power to live on. But, yet again, poor Ānanda was simply not up to the occasion, did not understand, and, therefore, did not ask the Buddha to remain with the Sangha until the end of this historical era. It was an omission for which some members of the early Sangha blamed Ānanda – a poor reward for the years of devoted service to his master, which the Buddha himself certainly appreciated. But when the Buddha had dropped his hint, Ānanda did not see its significance, made a polite and noncommittal rejoinder, and went off to sit at the foot of a nearby tree.

For a while, perhaps, even the Buddha may have had a fleeting wish for a companion who could understand more fully what was in his mind, as he felt his life ebbing away, because just at this point, Māra, his shadow-self, appeared. 'Let the Tathāgata achieve his *parinibbāṇa* now,' Māra whispered seductively. Why go on? He deserved his final rest; there was no point in further struggle. For the last time, the Buddha repelled Māra. He would not enter the bliss of his Final Nibbāṇa until his mission was complete and he was certain that the Order and the holy life were properly established. But, he added, that would be very soon: 'In three months time,' he told Māra, 'the Tathāgata will attain his *parinibbāṇa*.'[20]

It was then, the scriptures tell us, at the Capala Shrine in Vesālī, that the Buddha consciously and deliberately 'abandoned the will to live.'[21] It was a decision that reverberated throughout the cosmos. The world of men was shaken by an earthquake, which made even Ānanda realize that something momentous was afoot, and in the heavens a solemn drum began to beat. It was too late, the Buddha told the now contrite Ānanda, for his attendant to beg him to live on. He must now speak to the Sangha and bid his monks a formal farewell.

In the great painted hall of the Vesālī *ārāma*, he spoke to all the *bhikkhus* who were residing in the neighborhood. He had nothing new to tell them. 'I have only taught you things that I have experienced fully for myself,' he said. He had taken nothing on trust and they too must make the Dhamma a reality for themselves. They must thoroughly learn all the truths he had imparted, make them, by means of meditation, a living experience, so that they too knew them with the 'direct knowledge' of a yogin. Above all, they must live for others. The holy life had not been devised simply to benefit the enlightened, and Nibbāṇa was not a prize which any *bhikkhu* could selfishly keep to himself. They must live the Dhamma 'for the sake of the people, for the welfare and happiness of the multitude, out of compassion for the whole world, and for the good and well-being of gods and men.'[22]

The next morning, after the Buddha and Ānanda had begged for their food in the town, the Buddha turned round and gazed for a long time at Vesālī; it was the last time that he would ever see it. They then took the path to the village of Bhaṇḍagāma. From this point, the Buddha's wanderings seemed to be heading off the map of the civilized world. After he had stayed for a while in Bhaṇḍagāma, instructing the *bhikkhus* there, the Buddha traveled with Ānanda slowly northward, through the villages of Hatthigāma, Ambagāma, Jambugāma and Bhoganagama (all of which have disappeared without trace) until he arrived at Pāvā, where he lodged in the grove belonging to one Cunda, the son of a goldsmith. Cunda did homage to the Buddha, listened attentively to his instruction and then invited him to an excellent dinner, which included some *sūkaramaddava* ('pigs' soft food'). Nobody is quite sure what this dish really was: some of the commentaries say that it was succulent pork already on sale in the market (the Buddha never ate the flesh of an animal that had been killed especially for him); others argue that it was either a form of minced pork or a dish of the truffle mushrooms enjoyed by pigs. Some maintain that it was a special elixir, which Cunda, who was afraid that the Buddha would die and attain his *parinibbāṇa* that day, believed would prolong his life indefinitely.[23] At all events, the Buddha insisted on eating the *sūkaramaddava* and told the *bhikkhus* to eat the other food on the table. When he had finished, he told Cunda to bury what was left, since nobody – not even a god – could digest it. This could simply be an adverse appraisal of Cunda's culinary skills, but some modern scholars have suggested that the Buddha realized that the *sūkkaramaddava* had been poisoned: they see the loneliness of the Buddha's end and the remoteness of the location as a sign of a distance between the Buddha and the Sangha and believe that, like the two old kings, he too died a violent death.[24]

The Pāli texts, however, do not even consider this appalling possibility. The Buddha's request that Cunda bury the food was strange, but he had been ill for some time and expected to die shortly. That night he began to vomit blood and was gripped by a violent pain, but yet again he mastered his illness and set off with Ānanda to Kusinārā. He was now in the republic of Malla, whose inhabitants do not seem to have been interested in the Buddha's ideas. The texts tell us that he was accompanied by the usual retinue of monks, but apart from Ānanda, no senior member of the Order was with him. On his way to Kusinārā, the Buddha became tired and asked for some water. Even though the stream was stagnant and muddy, the water became clear as soon as Ānanda approached it with the Buddha's bowl. The scriptures emphasize such incidents to mitigate the bleak solitude of these last days. We hear that on the final leg of his journey, the Buddha converted a passing Mallian, who, fittingly, had been a follower of his old teacher, Alārā Kālāma. This man was so impressed by the quality of the Buddha's concentration that he made the Triple Refuge on the spot and presented the Buddha and Ānanda with two robes made of cloth of gold. But when the Buddha put his on, Ānanda exclaimed that it looked quite dull beside the brightness of his skin: the Buddha explained that this was a sign that he would very shortly – when he reached Kusinārā – achieve his Final Nibbāṇa. A little later, he told Ānanda that nobody should blame Cunda for his death: it was an act of great merit to give a Buddha his last almsfood before he attained his *parinibbāṇa.*[25]

What was this *parinibbāṇa*? Was it simply an extinction? And if so, why was this Nothingness regarded as such a glorious achievement? How would this 'final' Nibbāṇa differ from the peace that the Buddha had attained under the bodhi tree? The word *nibbāṇa,* it will be recalled, means 'cooling off' or 'going out,' like a flame. The term for the attainment of Nibbāṇa in this life in the texts is *sa-upādi-sesa.* An Arahant had extinguished the fires of craving, hatred and ignorance, but he still had a 'residue' (*sesa*) of 'fuel' (*upādi*) as long as he lived in the body, used his senses and mind, and experienced emotions. There was a potential for a further conflagration. But when an Arahant died, these *khandha* could never be ignited again, and could not feed the flame of a new existence.[26] The Arahant was, therefore, free from *saṃsāra* and could be absorbed wholly into the peace and immunity of Nibbāṇa.

But what did that mean? We have seen that the Buddha always refused to define Nibbāṇa, because we have no terms that are adequate for this experience that transcends the reach of the senses and the mind. Like those monotheists who preferred to speak of God in negative terms, the Buddha sometimes preferred to explain what Nibbāṇa was *not.* It was, he told his disciples, a state

> where there is neither earth nor water, light nor air; neither infinity or space; it is not infinity of reason but nor is it an absolute void . . . it is neither this world or another world; it is both sun and moon.[27]

That did not mean that it was really 'nothing'; we have seen that it became a Buddhist heresy to claim that an Arahant ceased to exist in Nibbāṇa. But it was an existence beyond the self, and blissful because there was no selfishness. Those of us who are unenlightened, and whose horizons are still constricted by egotism, cannot imagine this state. But those who had achieved the death of the ego knew that selflessness was not a void. When the Buddha tried to give his disciples a hint of what this peaceful Eden in the heart of the psyche was like, he mixed negative with positive terms. Nibbāṇa was, he said, 'the extinction of greed, hatred and delusion'; it was the Third Noble Truth; it was 'Taintless,' 'Unweakening,' 'Undisintegrating,' 'Inviolable,' 'Non-distress,' 'Non-affliction,' and 'Unhostility.' All these epithets emphasized that Nibbāṇa canceled out everything that we find intolerable in life. It was not a state of annihilation: it was 'Deathless.' But there were positive things that could be said of Nibbāṇa too: it was 'the Truth,' 'the Subtle,' 'the Other Shore,' 'the Everlasting,' 'Peace,' 'the Superior Goal,' 'Safety,' 'Purity, Freedom, Independence, the Island, the Shelter, the Harbor, the Refuge, the Beyond.'[28] It was *the* supreme good of humans and gods alike, an incomprehensible Peace, and an utterly safe refuge. Many of these images are reminiscent of words that monotheists have used to describe God.

Indeed, Nibbāṇa was very much like the Buddha himself. Later Buddhists of the Mahāyāna school would claim that he was so wholly infused by Nibbāṇa that he was identical with it. Just as Christians see what God might be like when they contemplate the man Jesus, these Buddhists could see the Buddha as the human expression of this state. Even in his own life, people had intimations of this. The *brahmin* who could not classify the Buddha, since he no longer fit into any mundane or celestial category, had sensed that, like Nibbāṇa, the Buddha was 'Something Else.' The Buddha had told him that he was 'one who had woken up,' a man who had shed the dreary, painful limitations of profane humanity and achieved something Beyond. King Pasenedi had also seen the Buddha as a refuge, a place of safety and purity. When he had left home, he had experimented with his human nature until he discovered this new region of peace within. But he was not unique. Anybody who applied himself or herself seriously to the holy life could find this Edenic serenity within. The Buddha had lived for forty-five years as a human without egotism; he had, therefore, been able to live with pain. But now that he was approaching the end of his life, he was about to shed the last indignities of age; the *khandha*, the 'bundles of firewood' that had blazed with greed and delusion in his youth, had long been extinguished, and could now be thrown away. He was about to reach the Other Shore. So he walked feebly but with great confidence toward the obscure little town where he would attain the *parinibbāṇa.*

The Buddha and Ānanda, two old men, crossed the Hiraññavatī river with their crowd of *bhikkhus,* and turned into a grove of sāl trees on the road that led into Kusinārā. By now the Buddha was in pain. He lay down and the sāl trees immediately burst into flower and dropped their petals upon him, even though it was not the season for blossom. The place was filled with gods, the Buddha said, who had come to witness his last triumph. But what gave a Buddha far more honor was the fidelity of his followers to the Dhamma he had brought them.

As he lay dying, the Buddha gave directions about his funeral. His ashes were to be treated like those of a *cakkavatti;* his body should be wrapped in a cloth and cremated with perfumed woods, and the remains buried at the crossroads of a great city. From first to last, the Buddha had been paired with the *cakkavatti,* and after his enlightenment had offered the world an alternative to a power based on aggression and coercion. His funeral arrangements drew attention to this ironic counterpoint. The great kings of the region, who had appeared to be so potent when the young Gotama had arrived in Magadha and Kosala, had both been snuffed out. The violence and cruelty of their deaths showed that the monarchies were fueled by selfishness, greed, ambition, envy, hatred and destruction. They had brought prosperity and cultural advancement; they represented the march of progress and benefited many people. But there was another way of life that did not have to impose itself so violently, that was not dedicated to self-aggrandizement, and that made men and women happier and more humane.

The funeral arrangements were just too much for Ānanda. His plight during these last days reminds us of the immense gulf that separates the unenlightened from the Arahant. Ānanda knew all about Buddhism intellectually, but this knowledge was no substitute for the 'direct knowledge' of the yogin. It could be of no help to him when he started to experience the pain of the loss of his master. This was infinitely worse than the death of Sāriputta. He understood the Noble Truth of Suffering with his mundane, rational mind, but he had not absorbed it so that it fused with his whole being. He still could not accept the fact that everything was transient and would pass away. Because he was not a proficient yogin, he could not 'penetrate' these doctrines and make them a living reality. Instead of feeling a yogic certainty, he felt only raw pain. After he had listened to the Buddha's unimpassioned directions about his ashes, Ānanda left his master's bedside and fled to one of the other huts in the grove. For a long time, he stood weeping, resting his head against the lintel. He felt a complete failure: 'I am still only a beginner,' wept the elderly *bhikkhu.* 'I have not reached the goal of the holy life; my quest is unfulfilled.' He lived in a community of spiritual giants who had reached Nibbāṇa. Who would help him now? Who would even bother with him? 'My Teacher is about to attain his *parinibbāṇa* – my compassionate Teacher who was always kind to me.'

When the Buddha heard about Ānanda's tears, he sent for him. 'That is enough, Ānanda,' he said. 'Don't be sorrowful; don't grieve.' Had he not explained, over and over again, that nothing was permanent but that separation was the law of life? 'And Ānanda,' the Buddha concluded, 'for years you have waited on me with constant love and kindness. You have taken care of my physical needs, and have supported me in all your words and thoughts. You have done all this to help me, joyfully and with your whole heart. You have earned merit, Ānanda. Keep trying, and you will soon be enlightened too.'[29]

But Ānanda was still struggling. 'Lord,' he cried, 'do not go to your Final Rest in this dreary little town, with mud walls; this heathen, jungle outpost, this backwater.' The Buddha had spent the greater part of his working life in such great cities as Rājagaha, Kosambī, Sāvattī, and Vārānasī. Why could he not return to one of these cities, and finish his quest surrounded by all his noble disciples, instead of dying here alone, among these ignorant unbelievers? The texts show that the early Sangha was embarrassed by the obscurity of Kusinārā and the fact that their Teacher died far away in the jungle. The Buddha tried to cheer Ānanda, pointing out that Kusinārā had once been a thriving city and the great capital of a *cakkavatti.* But the Buddha's choice of Kusinārā almost certainly had a deeper reason. No Buddhist could ever rest on past achievements; the Sangha must always press forward to bring help to the wider world. And a Buddha would not see a dismal little town like Kusinārā in the same way as would an unenlightened man. For years he had trained his conscious and his unconscious mind to see reality from an entirely different perspective, free from the distorting aura of egotism that clouds the judgment of most human beings. He did not need the external prestige upon which many of us rely in order to prop up our sense of self. As a Tathāgata, his egotism had 'gone.' A Buddha had no time to think of himself, even on his deathbed. Right up to the last, he continued to live for others, inviting the Mallians of Kusinārā to come to the grove in order to share his triumph. He also took the time to instruct a passing mendicant, who belonged to another sect but was drawn to the Buddha's teaching, even though Ānanda protested that the Buddha was ill and exhausted.

Finally, he turned back to Ānanda, able with his usual sympathy to enter into his thoughts. 'You may be thinking, Ānanda: "The word of the Teacher is now a thing of the past; now we have no more Teacher." But that is not how you should see it. Let the Dhamma and the Discipline that I have taught you be your Teacher when I am gone.'[30] He had always told his followers to look not at him but at the Dhamma; he himself had never been important. Then he turned to the crowd of *bhikkhus* who had accompanied him on this last journey, and reminded them yet again that 'All individual things pass away. Seek your liberation with diligence.'[31]

Having given his last advice to his followers, the Buddha fell into a coma. Some of the monks felt able to trace his journey through the higher states of consciousness that he had explored so often in meditation. But he had gone beyond any state known to human beings whose minds are still dominated by sense experience. While the gods rejoiced, the earth shook and those *bhikkhus* who had not yet achieved enlightenment wept, the Buddha experienced an extinction that was, paradoxically, the supreme state of being and the final goal of humanity:

> As a flame blown out by the wind
> Goes to rest and cannot be defined,
> So the enlightened man freed from selfishness
> Goes to rest and cannot be defined.
> Gone beyond all images –
> Gone beyond the power of words.[32]

NOTES

INTRODUCTION

1. *Majjhima Nikāya,* 89.

1. RENUNCIATION

1. The date of Gotama's birth and 'Going Forth' are now disputed. Western scholars once imagined that he had been born in about 563 and would, therefore, have left home in about 534, but recent scholarship indicates that Gotama could have left home as late as 450 B.C.E. Heinz Berchant, 'The Date of the Buddha reconsidered,' *Indologia Taurinensin,* 10.
2. Gotama's son was called Rāhula, which has traditionally been understood to mean 'fetter.' Some modern scholarship has questioned this derivation.
3. *Majjhima Nikāya,* 36, 100.
4. Ibid., 26, 36, 85, 100.
5. *Jātaka,* I:62
6. Luke 9:57–62; 14:25–27; 18:28–30.
7. *Majjhima Nikāya,* 26.
8. *Aṇguttara Nikāya,* 3:38.
9. Mircea Eliade, *The Myth of the Eternal Return or Cosmos and History,* (trans. Willard J. Trask), Princeton, NJ, 1954.

10. *Majjhima Nikāya*, 26.
11. *Udāna*, 8:3.
12. *Sutta-Nipāta*, 3:1.
13. Karl Jaspers, *The Origin and Goal of History*, trans. Michael Bullock, London, 1953.
14. Ibid., 2–12.
15. Ibid., 7, 13.
16. Ibid., 28–46.
17. Genesis 2–3.
18. Joseph Campbell, *Oriental Mythology, The Masks of God*, New York, 1962, 211–18.
19. Vinaya: *Cullavagga*, 6:4; 7:1.
20. *Majjhima Nikāya*, 4.
21. Alfred Weber, *Kulturgeschichte als Kultursoziologie*, Leiden, 1935; *Das Tragische und die Geschichte*, Hamburg, 1943 passim.
22. Richard F. Gombrich, *Theravāda Buddhism: A Social History from Ancient Benares to Modern Columbo*, London and New York, 1988, 33–59.
23. Ibid., 33–34; Hermann Oldenberg, *The Buddha: His Life, His Doctrine, His Order* (trans. William Hoey), London, 1882, 19–21, 44–48; Trevor Ling, *The Buddha: Buddhist Civilization in India and Ceylon*, London, 1973, 66–67.
24. Sukumar Dutt, *Buddhist Monks and Monasteries of India*, London, 1962, 73.
25. Jaspers, *Origin and Goal*, 48–49.
26. Ibid., 55.
27. Marshall G. S. Hodgson, *The Venture of Islam, Conscience and History in a World Civilization*, 3 vols., Chicago and London, 1974, vol. I, 108–35.
28. Ling, *The Buddha*, 38–55; Michael Carrithers, *The Buddha*, Oxford and New York, 1983, 13–18; Gombrich, *Theravāda Buddhism*, 50–59.

29. Ling, *The Buddha,* 48–49.
30. Gombrich, *Theravāda Buddhism,* 349–50; Carrithers, *The Buddha,* 12–14.
31. Ling, *The Buddha,* 53–63; Michael Edwardes, *In the Blowing Out of a Flame: The World of the Buddha and the World of Man,* London, 1976, 27–29.
32. Richard F. Gombrich, *How Buddhism Began: The Conditioned Genesis of the Early Teachings,* London and Atlantic Highlands, NJ, 1996, 31–33; *Theravāda Buddhism,* 46–48; Carrithers, *The Buddha,* 24–25; Ling, *The Buddha,* 47–52.
33. Ling, *The Buddha,* 65–66; Oldenberg, *The Buddha,* 41–44.
34. *Chandogya Upaniṣad,* 6:13.
35. Oldenberg, *The Buddha,* 59–60.
36. Ibid., 64; Campbell, *Oriental Mythology: The Masks of God,* 197–98.
37. Dutt, *Buddhist Monks,* 38–40.
38. *Jātaka* I, 54–65 in Henry Clarke Warren, *Buddhism in Translation,* Cambridge, Mass., 1900, 48–67.
39. *Dīgha Nikāya* 2:21–29.
40. *Jātaka* I:54.
41. Ibid., I:61.
42. Ibid., I:63.

2. QUEST

1. *Sutta-Nipāta* 3:1.
2. Trevor Ling, *The Buddha: Buddhist Civilization in India and Ceylon,* London, 1973, 76–82; Hermann Oldenberg, *The Buddha: His Life, His Doctrine, His Order* (trans. William Hoey) London, 1882, 66–71; Michael Carrithers, *The Buddha,* Oxford and New York, 1983, 18–23; Sukumar Dutt, *Buddhist Monks and Monasteries in India,* London, 1962, 38–50.
3. Ling, *The Buddha,* 77–78.

4. Richard F. Gombrich, *Theravāda Buddhism: A Social History from Ancient Benares to Modern Columbo,* London and New York, 1988, 47.
5. Ibid., 48–49.
6. Oldenburg, *The Buddha,* 67.
7. Carrithers, *The Buddha,* 25.
8. Ling, *The Buddha,* 78–82; Joseph Campbell, *Oriental Mythology: The Masks of God,* New York, 1962, 218–34.
9. Ling, *The Buddha,* 92; Mircea Eliade, *Yoga, Immortality and Freedom* (trans. William J. Trask), London, 1958, 102.
10. Sāṃkhya Karita, 59.
11. Eliade, *Yoga,* 8–35.
12. *Majjhima Nikāya,* 26, 36, 85, 100.
13. Eliade, *Yoga,* 35–114, for a discussion of classical yoga.
14. Ibid., 4–5.
15. Galatians, 4:1–11.
16. Genesis 18 cf. The Acts of the Apostles 14:11–17, where the people of Lystra think that Paul and Barnabas were epiphanies of the gods Zeus and Hermes.
17. Isaiah 6:5.
18. Jeremiah 44:15–19.
19. Ezekiel, 4:4–17; 12; 24:15–24.
20. Eliade, *Yoga,* 59–62.
21. Yoga-Suttas 2:42.
22. Eliade, *Yoga,* 53–55.
23. Ibid., 55–58.
24. Ibid., 56.
25. Ibid., 47–49.
26. Ibid., 68–69.
27. Ibid., 70–71.
28. Ibid., 72–76; 167–73; Carrithers, *The Buddha,* 32–33; Edward Conze, *Buddhist Meditation,* London, 1956, 20–22.

29. Carrithers, *The Buddha,* 30, 34–35.

30. Ibid., 33; Eliade, *Yoga,* 77–84.

31. Karen Armstrong, *A History of God,* London and New York, 1993.

32. *Majjhima Nikāya,* 26, 36, 85, 100.

33. Ibid.

34. Ibid., 12, 36, 85, 200.

35. Ibid., 36.

36. Ibid.

3. ENLIGHTENMENT

1. Joseph Campbell, *Oriental Mythology: The Masks of God,* New York, 1962, 236.

2. *Majjhima Nikāya,* 36.

3. Ibid.

4. *Aṇguttara Nikāya* 9:3; Majjhima Nikāya, 38, 41.

5. *Majjhima Nikāya,* 27, 38, 39, 112.

6. Ibid., 100.

7. *Dīgha Nikāya,* 327.

8. *Saṁyutta Nikāya,* 2:36.

9. Vinaya: *Mahāvagga,* 1:6.

10. *Udana,* 3:10.

11. *Majjhima Nikāya,* 38.

12. Ibid.

13. *Majjhima Nikāya,* 2.

14. Hermann Oldenberg, *The Buddha: His Life, His Doctrine, His Order* (trans. William Hoey), London, 1882, 299–302; Edward Conze, *Buddhism: Its Essence and Development,* Oxford, 1957, 102.

15. *Aṇguttara Nikāya,* 8:7:3; Richard F. Gombrich, *How Buddhism Began: The Conditioned Genesis of the Early Teachings,* London and Atlantic Highlands, NJ, 1996, 60–61.

16. Michael Carrithers, *The Buddha,* Oxford and New York, 1983, 75–77.
17. *Aṅguttara Nikāya,* 8:20.
18. *Majjhima Nikāya,* 100.
19. Ibid., 36; *Saṁyutta Nikāya,* 12:65.
20. *Saṁyutta Nikāya,* 12:65.
21. *Majjhima Nikāya,* 36.
22. Vinaya: *Mahāvagga,* 1:5.
23. *Dīgha Nikāya,* 1:182.
24. *Majjhima Nikāya,* 36.
25. *Aṅguttara Nikāya,* 10:95.
26. Oldenberg, *The Buddha,* 279–82.
27. *Sutta-Nipāta,* 5:7.
28. *Jātaka,* 1:68–76; Henry Clarke Warren, *Buddhism in Translation,* Cambridge, Mass., 1900, 71–83.
29. *Jātaka,* 1:70.
30. Ibid., 1:71.
31. Mircea Eliade, *The Sacred and the Profane: The Nature of Religion* (trans. Willard R. Trask), New York and London, 1957, 33–37; 52–54; 169. Joseph Campbell, *The Hero With a Thousand Faces,* Princeton, NJ, 1986 edn., 40–46, 56–58; *The Power of Myth* (with Bill Moyers), New York, 1988, 160–62.
32. *Jātaka,* 1:72.
33. Ibid., 1:73.
34. Ibid., 1:74.
35. Ibid., 1:75.
36. Vinaya: *Mahāvagga,* 1:4.
37. Ibid., 1:5.
38. Ibid.
39. Eliade, *Sacred and Profane,* 200; Campbell, *The Power of Myth,* 174–75.
40. Vinaya: *Mahāvagga,* 1:5.

41. Ibid.
42. Ibid., 1:6.

4. ĐHAMMA

1. Vinaya: *Mahāvagga,* 1:6.
2. Ibid.
3. Ibid.
4. *Majjhima Nikāya,* 22.
5. *Saṁyutta Nikāya,* 53:31.
6. *Majjhima Nikāya,* 63.
7. Vinaya: *Mahāvagga,* 1:6; *Saṁyutta Nikāya,* 56:11.
8. Ibid.
9. According to Buddhist legend in the later commentaries, Kondañña was the *brahmin* who came to examine the infant Gotama, and prophesied that he would become a Buddha. Because of his conversion experience, he was always known as Aññāta Kondañña: Kondañña who knows.
10. Vinaya: *Mahāvagga,* 1:6.
11. Ibid.
12. Ibid. These first Buddhists, we are told, graduated at once from 'stream-enterers,' with only seven lives ahead, to Arahants, fully enlightened human beings who are liberated from *saṃsāra.* Later tradition taught that there were two intermediate steps for most people: [1] the 'once-returner' (*sakadāgāmi*) with only one earthly life left, and [2] the 'never-returner,' (*anāgāmi*), who will only be reborn in heaven as a god.
13. *Majjhima Nikāya,* 26. Tillman Vetter, *The Ideas and Meditative Practices of Early Buddhism,* London, New York, Copenhagen and Cologne, 1986, xxix.
14. Vinaya: *Mahāvagga,* 1:6.

15. *Saṁyutta Nikāya*, 12:65; *Dīgha Nikāya*, 14; Vinaya: *Mahāvagga*, 1:1; *Udāna*, 1:1-3.
16. Vinaya: *Mahāvagga*, 1:1.
17. Michael Carrithers, *The Buddha*, Oxford and New York, 1983, 68–70; Hermann Oldenberg, *The Buddha: His Life, His Doctrine, His Order*, (trans. William Hoey), London, 1882, 224–52; Karl Jaspers, *The Great Philosophers: The Foundations* (trans. Ralph Meinheim), London, 1962, 39–40; Vetter, *Ideas and Meditative Practices*, 240–42.
18. Richard F. Gombrich, *Theravāda Buddhism: A Social History from Ancient Benares to Modern Columbo*, London and New York, 1988, 62–63; Oldenberg, *The Buddha*, 240–42; Carrithers, *The Buddha*, 66.
19. Vetter, *Ideas and Meditative Practices*, 50–52; Oldenberg, *The Buddha*, 243–47.
20. Vetter, *Ideas and Meditative Practices*, 49–50.
21. Oldenberg, *The Buddha*, 248–51; Carrithers, *The Buddha*, 57–58.
22. *Aṇguttara Nikāya*, 6:63.
23. Vinaya: *Mahāvagga*, 1:6; *Saṁyutta Nikāya*, 22:59.
24. Ibid.
25. *Saṁyutta Nikāya*, 12:61.
26. *Dīgha Nikāya*, 9.
27. Vinaya: *Mahāvagga*, 1:6.
28. Ibid.
29. *Mājjhima Nikāya*, 1.
30. Vinaya: *Mahāvagga*, 1:7.
31. Ibid.
32. Ibid, 1:8. In fact, scholars believe that during the Buddha's lifetime, disciples simply made a 'Single Refuge' to the Buddha alone and that the Triple Refuge did not become customary until after the Buddha's death.

33. Vinaya: *Mahāvagga*, 1:11.
34. Sukumar Dutt, *Buddhist Monks and Monasteries of India*, London, 1962, 33.

5. MISSION

1. *Saṁyutta Nikāya*, 22:87.
2. Andrew Skilton, *A Concise History of Buddhism*, Birmingham, U.K., 1994, 19.
3. Vinaya: *Cullavagga*. 6:4.
4. Vinaya: *Mahāvagga*, 1:12; Sukumar Dutt, *Buddhist Monks and Monasteries of India*, London, 1962, 22.
5. Vinaya: *Mahāvagga*, 1:13.
6. Ibid., 1:14–20.
7. Mircea Eliade, *Yoga, Immortality and Freedom* (trans. Willard R. Trask), London, 1958, 85–90.
8. *Sutta-Nipāta*, 136; *Udāna*, 1:4.
9. Vinaya: *Mahāvagga*, 1:20.
10. Ibid., 1:21; *Saṁyutta Nikāya*, 35:28.
11. Richard F. Gombrich, *Theravāda Buddhism: A Social History from Ancient Benares to Modern Columbo*, London and New York, 1988, 65–69.
12. Vinaya: *Mahāvagga*, 1:21.
13. Ibid., 1:22.
14. Ibid., 1:23.
15. Edward Conze, *Buddhism: Its Essence and Development*, Oxford, 1957, 91–92.
16. Vinaya: *Mahāvagga*, 1:24.
17. *Jātaka*, 1:87; Commentary on the *Aṇguttara Nikāya*, 1:302; Edward J. Thomas, *The Life of Buddha in Legend and History*, London, 1969, 97–102; Bhikkhu Ñānamoli (trans. and ed.), *The Life of the Buddha, According to the Pāli Canon*, Kandy, Sri Lanka, 1972, 75–77.

18. Thomas, *Life of Buddha*, 102–3.
19. Vinaya: *Cullavagga*, 6:4; *Saṁyutta Nikāya*, 10:8.
20. Trevor Ling, *The Buddha: Buddhist Civilization in India and Ceylon*, London, 1973, 46–47.
21. Vinaya: *Cullavagga*, 6:4; *Saṁyutta Nikāya*, 10:8.
22. Dutt, *Buddhist Monks*, 58.
23. Vinaya: *Mahāvagga*, 3:1.
24. Ibid., 8:27.
25. Vinaya: *Cullavagga*, 6:5–9.
26. *Majjhima Nikāya*, 128; Vinaya: *Mahavagga*, 10:4.
27. *Majjhima Nikāya*, 89.
28. Ling, *The Buddha*, 140–52; Michael Edwardes, *In the Blowing Out of a Flame: The World of the Buddha and the World of Man*, London, 1976, 30–31.
29. Gombrich, *Theravāda Buddhism*, 81–86; Michael Carrithers, *The Buddha*, Oxford and New York, 1983, 95–97.
30. *Dīgha Nikāya*, 3:191.
31. *Majjhima Nikāyu*, 143.
32. Ling, *The Buddha*, 135–37; Gombrich, *Theravāda Buddhism*, 75–77.
33. Carrithers, *The Buddha*, 86–87.
34. Gombrich, *Theravāda Buddhism*, 78.
35. *Aṇguttara Nikāya*, 2:69–70.
36. *Dīgha Nikāya*, 3:180–83.
37. *Aṇguttara Nikāya*, 4:43–45.
38. *Saṁyutta Nikāya*, 3:1–8.
39. Shabbat 31A; cf. Matthew 7:12; Confucius, *Analects* 12:2.
40. *Aṇguttara Nikāya*, 3:65.
41. Ibid.
42. Ibid.
43. *Sutta-Nipāta*, 118.
44. Vinaya: *Cullavagga*, 10:1.

45. *Dīgha Nikāya*, 16; Isalene Blew Horner, *Women Under Primitive Buddhism*, London, 1930, 287.
46. Rita M. Gross, 'Buddhism,' in Jean Holm with John Bowker (eds.), *Women in Religion*, London, 1994, 5–6; Anne Bancroft, 'Women in Buddhism,' in Ursula King (ed.), *Women in the World's Religions, Past and Present*, New York, 1987, passim.
47. *Dīgha Nikāya*, 16.
48. Leila Ahmed, *Women and Gender in Islam*, New Haven and London, 1992, 11–29.
49. *Majjhima Nikāya*, 128,
50. *Dhammapada*, 5–6.
51. Vinaya: *Mahāvagga*, 10:5.
52. Dutt, *Buddhist Monks*, 66.
53. *Dhammapada*, 183–85.
54. Gombrich, *Theravāda Buddhism*, 92; Oldenberg, *The Buddha: His Life, His Doctrine, His Order* (trans. William Hoey), London, 1882, xxxiii.
55. Gombrich, *Theravāda Buddhism*, 88–89.
56. *Aṇguttara Nikāya*, 4:36.

6. PARINIBBĀṆA

1. *Saṁyutta Nikāya*, 3:25.
2. *Majjhima Nikāya*, 89.
3. Bhikkhu Ñānamoli (trans. and ed.), *The Life of the Buddha, According to the Pāli Canon*, Kandy, Sri Lanka, 1972, 285. (This story is in the commentaries and not in the Canon.)
4. *Majjhima Nikāya*, 104.
5. Vinaya: *Cullavagga*, 7:2.
6. Ibid., 7:3.
7. Ibid.
8. Ibid.
9. Ibid.

10. Ibid.
11. Ibid.
12. Ibid., 7:5.
13. *Dīgha Nikāya*, 16.
14. Ibid.
15. Ibid.
16. Ibid.
17. Ibid.; *Saṁyutta Nikāya*, 47:9.
18. *Dīgha Nikāya*, 16; *Aṇguttara Nikāya*, 8:10.
19. Ibid., 47:14.
20. *Dīgha Nikāya*, 16; *Aṇguttara Nikāya*, 8:10.
21. *Dīgha Nikāya*, 16.
22. Ibid.
23. Ñānamoli, *Life of Buddha*, 357–58.
24. Michael Edwardes, *In the Blowing Out of a Flame: The World of the Buddha and the World of Man*, London, 1976, 45.
25. *Dīgha Nikāya*, 16.
26. Richard F. Gombrich, *Theravāda Buddhism: A Social History from Ancient Benares to Modern Columbo*, London and New York, 1988, 65–69.
27. *Udāna*, 8:1.
28. *Saṁyutta Nikāya*, 43:1–44.
29. *Dīgha Nikāya*, 16.
30. Ibid.; *Aṇguttara Nikāya*, 76.
31. *Dīgha Nikāya*, 16; *Aṇguttara Nikāya*, 4:76.
32. *Sutta-Nipāta*, 5:7.

GLOSSARY

Ahimsā: 'Harmlessness'; the ethic adopted by many of the ascetics of North India to counter the aggression of the new states.

Akusala: 'Unskillful' or 'unhelpful' states, which will impede the quest for Enlightenment.

Anattā: 'No-Soul'; the doctrine that denies the existence of a constant, stable and discrete personality.

Arahant: An 'Accomplished One,' who has attained Nibbāṇa.

Arāmā: Pleasure-park donated to the Buddhist Order for a settlement.

Āsana: The correct position for yogic meditation, with straight back and crossed legs.

Avāsā: Rural settlements, often built from scratch each year by the Buddhist monks, for the monsoon retreats.

Ātman: The eternal, unchangeable Self sought by the yogins, ascetics and followers of the Sāṃkhya philosophy. It was believed in the *Upaniṣads* to be identical with *brahman.*

Āyatana: Meditative planes achieved by a very advanced yogin.

Bhikkhu: An 'almsman,' a mendicant monk who begs for his daily food; the feminine form is **bhikkhunī:** nun.

Bodhisatta: A man or woman who is destined to achieve enlightenment. Sanskrit: *boddhisatva.*

Brahman: The fundamental, supreme and absolute principle of the cosmos in Vedic and Upaniṣadic religion.

Brahmin: A member of the priestly caste in Āryan society, responsible for sacrifice and the transmission of the Vedas.

Brahmacariya: The holy life of chastity, the quest for enlightenment and liberation from pain.

Buddha: An Enlightened or Awakened person.

Cakkavatti: The World Ruler or Universal King of Indian folklore, who would govern the whole world and impose justice and righteousness by force.

Ceto-vimutti: The 'release of the mind'; a synonym for enlightenment and the achievement of Nibbāṇa.

Dhamma: Originally, the natural condition of things, their essence, the fundamental law of their existence; then: religious truth, the doctrines and practices that make up a particular religious system. Sanskrit: *dharma.*

Dhārāna: A yogic term: 'concentration.' A process of internal visualization, during which the yogin becomes conscious of his own consciousness.

Dukkha: 'Awry, flawed, unsatisfactory'; often simply translated as 'suffering.'

Ekāgratā: In yoga, the concentration of the mind 'on a single point.'

Gotamī: The name of any woman belonging to the Gotama tribe.

Iddhi: The dominion of spirit over matter; the 'miraculous' powers thought to come with proficiency in yoga, e.g., levitation or the ability to change shape at will.

Jhāna: A yogic trance; a current of unified thought that deepens in four distinct stages. Sanskrit: *dhyāna.*

Jina: A conqueror, an honorary title of Buddha, used by Jains.

Kamma: Actions; deeds. Sanskrit: *Karman.*

Khandha: 'Heaps, bundles, lumps'; the constituents of the human personality in the Buddha's theory of *anattā*. The five 'heaps' are body, feelings, perception, volition and consciousness.

Ksatriya: The caste of warriors, noblemen and aristocrats responsible in Āryan society for government and defense.

Kusala: The 'skillful' or 'helpful' states of mind and heart that Buddhists should cultivate in order to achieve enlightenment.

Nibbāṇa: 'Extinction; blowing out': the extinction of self which brings enlightenment and liberation from pain (*dukkha*). Sanskrit: *Nirvana.*

Nikāya: 'Collections' of discourses in the Pāli Canon.

Niyamas: The bodily and psychological disciplines which are a prerequisite for yogic meditation.

Pabbajjā: 'Going Forth'; the act of renouncing the world in order to live the holy life of a monk. Later, the first step in Buddhist ordination.

Pāli: The North Indian dialect used in the most important collection of Buddhist scriptures.

Parinibbāṇa: The 'Final Nibbāṇa'; the final rest of an enlightened person achieved at death, since he or she will not be reborn into another existence.

Pātimokkha: 'Bond'; a ceremony whereby the early monks came together every six years to recite the Buddhist Dhamma; later, after the Buddha's death, this became a recitation of the monastic rule of the Order and a confession of transgressions, which was held once a fortnight.

Praktṛi: Nature; the natural world in the philosophy of Sāṃkhya.

Prāṇāyāma: The breathing exercises of yoga, which induce a state of trance and well-being.

Pratyāhāra: In yoga, a 'withdrawal of the senses,' the ability to contemplate an object with the intellect alone.

Puruṣa: The Absolute Spirit that pervades all beings in the philosophy of Sāṃkhya.

Sakyamūni: 'The Sage of the Republic of Sakka,' a title given to the Buddha.

Samādhi: Yogic concentration; meditation; one of the components of the Eightfold Path to enlightenment.

Sāṃkhya: 'Discrimination': a philosophy, akin to yoga, which was first preached by the sage Kapila in the seventh century B.C.E.

Sammā Sambuddha: A Teacher of Enlightenment, one of whom comes to humanity every 32,000 years; Siddhatta Gotama is the Sammā Sambuddha of our own age.

Saṃsāra: 'Keeping going'; the cycle of death and rebirth, which propels people from one life to the next; the transience and restlessness of mundane existence.

Sangha: Originally a tribal assembly, an ancient governing body in the old republics of North India; later a sect professing the *dhamma* of a particular teacher; finally, the Buddhist Order of Bhikkhus.

Sankhāra: 'Formation'; the formative element in *kamma,* which determines and shapes one's next existence.

Sutta: A religious discourse. Sanskrit: *Sutra.*

Tanhā: The 'craving' or 'desire' which is the most powerful cause of suffering.

Tapas: Asceticism; self-mortification.

Tathāgata: 'Thus Gone,' the title given to the Buddha after enlightenment, sometimes translated as 'the Perfect One.'

Tipiṭaka: Literally 'Three Baskets,' the three main divisions of the Pāli Canon.

Upādāna: 'Clinging,' attachment; it is etymologically related to *upādi,* fuel.

Uposatha: The days of fasting and abstinence in the Vedic tradition.

Upaniṣad: The esoteric texts that developed a mystical and spiritualized understanding of the Vedas, and which would form the basis of Hinduism.

Vassa: The retreat during the monsoon rains from June to September.

Veda: The inspired texts, recited and interpreted by the *brahmins,* in the Āryan religious system.

Vinaya: The monastic code of the Buddhist Order; one of the 'Three Baskets' of the Tipiṭaka.

Vaiśya: The third caste of farmers and stockbreeders in the Āryan system.

Vāsanā: The subconscious activities of the mind.

Yama: The 'prohibitions' observed by yogins and ascetics, who were forbidden to steal, lie, have sex, take intoxicants or to kill or harm another being.

Yoga: The discipline of 'yoking' the powers of the mind in order to cultivate alternative states of consciousness and insight.

Yogin: A practitioner of yoga.

INDEX